D0581977

THE NEW GRANNY'S SURVIVAL GUIDE

To the gransnetters,
for their wisdom and wit.

Foreword by Janet Ellis

THE NEW GRANNY'S SURVIVAL GUIDE

EVERYTHING YOU NEED TO KNOW TO BE THE **BEST** GRAN

Vermilion
LONDON

5 7 9 10 8 6 4

First published in 2013 by Vermilion, an imprint of Ebury Publishing
A Random House Group company

The Random House Group Limited Reg. No. 954009

Addresses for companies within the Random House Group can be found
at www.randomhouse.co.uk

Penguin Random House is committed to a sustainable future for
our business, our readers and our planet. This book is made from
Forest Stewardship Council® certified paper.

Designed and set by seagulls.net

Printed and bound in Great Britain by Clays Ltd, St Ives plc

ISBN 9780091948146

The information in this book has been compiled by way of general guidance in relation to the specific subjects addressed, but is not a substitute and not to be relied on for medical, healthcare, pharmaceutical or other professional advice on specific circumstances and in specific locations. So far as the author is aware the information given is correct and up to date as at October 2013. Practice, laws and regulations all change, and the reader should obtain up to date professional advice on any such issues. The author and publishers disclaim, as far as the law allows, any liability arising directly or indirectly from the use, or misuse, of the information contained in this book.

CONTENTS

FOREWORD

Nine years ago, I was rushing into the special care baby unit of a London hospital, harassed and worried, when a lovely nurse stopped me. 'Steady, Mum,' she said, smiling, 'your baby will wait a few more minutes!' Not *my* baby, I told her, I'm visiting my daughter's child. My grandson. My new grandson. My *first* grandson. 'Congratulations, Grandma!' she said. Grandma? Me? Wow, it sounded good.

If I'm honest, when I learnt I was going to be a grandparent I did wonder if I might be granted extra wisdom at some point, or gain more – some? – patience (which would be useful all round for everyone). When Sonny arrived – nine weeks early as Sophie had developed pre-eclampsia, hence the need for special care – sadly, I hadn't suddenly acquired additional skills.

Raising my three children had been a big adventure. A proper 'without maps, some bumpy roads and unexpected diversions' type of journey, where we found all sorts of things and places and experiences together. It had mostly worked out – they're really nice people, anyway – but how would I be this time, at the start of a different path?

Both my grandmothers died when my parents were still teenagers, and I'd lost both my grandfathers by the time I was six. If I had any image in my mind of what grandparenting might involve, it was based on other people's tales: it was all very cosy, but remote. I was in my late forties when Sonny arrived, still working, still looking after my other two kids (my youngest was only twelve). Where were my role models when I needed them? I don't think I was *nervous*, exactly, but I could have done with a manual, or other people to talk to. Of which more later.

Two things were immediately apparent as I began my Unsupervised Grandma Training. Firstly, my relationship with my daughter suddenly shifted and deepened in an amazing way. This seemingly hardly-out-of-nappies-herself person now assumed the care of an infant. If I felt proud of her before (and I did, very), then seeing Sophie as a loving, thoughtful, energetic and imaginative mother is the icing on a very delicious cake. I love the way she brings up her boys (there are two more now, as it happens); she does some things differently, of course, but she involves me in what's happening and what they're doing all the time. We always talked, a lot, but chatting mother-to-mother is a revelation.

The other brilliant thing I discovered is that I get lots of second chances to do stuff. As well as the storytelling and painting kind of things (and don't tell me that a small child's unstinting admiration of your drawing skills isn't a lovely thing), there's the splashing in puddles and the simply-stopping-to-look style of behaviour small people are so good at. I'd forgotten, for example, how a simple walk in the park with a toddler is a wondrous event – every twig and stone warrants careful study. (Useful note: don't do this on a tight schedule, otherwise 'Come on, Mummy's waiting' might be the first words they learn, simply through repetition.)

Watching old films together never loses its appeal. Nor does laughing through our chaotic cooking experiments. Rediscovering books my kids loved is a treat, likewise the dizzyingly vast array of wonderful new ones. Enjoying babies all over again is gorgeous, then there's the super-lovely thing that they grow up into interesting, imaginative, funny kids ... I could go on (I usually do!). Plus – and apologies for treacle, but – there's also *so* much love.

Disadvantages? Not many. I don't like how I'm full of new fears for them. Not the predator on the streets – we've always needed to protect our children from that sort of thing, that's not different – but the world seems to be a lot sharper than it was. And higher up – how *did* I let my kids go up and down stairs or climb trees so blithely? Concrete seems harder and fire is hotter, I'm quite sure of it. Corners jut and glass threatens to splinter. If I could wrap the entire world in a protective coating, things wouldn't seem so daunting. The only good thing is that a chorus of little voices yell 'Don't be silly, Grandma!' when I try – weakly – to stop them behaving like the properly adventurous boys they are.

If I can't quite keep up with their toys and crazes (Pokémon? Ben 10? Moshi Monsters? Me neither), I can supply a carefully hoarded store of toys that Mummy and Uncle Jack and Auntie Martha played with.

While being woken at six o'clock (thanks, Kit) never gets easier and retrieving far-flung toys and food (yours, I think, Ray) is still a chore, if the pedantry of a nine-year-old makes me just as irritated as it ever did (Sonny, that's enough), I still don't quite get the 'At least you can hand them back' thing. I always feel a little disconsolate when they leave ... but a glass of wine (yes, okay, an *uninterrupted* glass of wine) usually helps!

It's an ongoing project, this grandma lark – quite well structured, with a good reward scheme and a promising future. Up till recently, all that was missing was a proper, nationwide support network. When I say 'all', I mean, 'How come it took so long?' and 'There's no need to ever be without it from now on'. In this fast-paced, geographically spread, diversely aged new era of grandparenting, thank heavens for Gransnet. We all need reassurance, advice and the opportunity to share (I know I do), and it's fantastic that all that good sense and good cheer is harnessed so well in one place.

By the way, when I told that nurse I was Grandma not Mum, she also said 'Oh, you lucky woman!' And she was right, I am. Now, can I show you some photos of the grandboys ...?

Janet Ellis

INTRODUCTION

'Gransnet is the best help button ever – someone always seems to have the answer!' (ganja)

If your image of grans is a bunch of grey-haired knitting obsessives, then think again. Times have changed. Now you're as likely to find an octogenarian on an iPad as you are to see them tucked up in a rocking chair in front of the fire. You'll find just as many grandparents as parents at the school gates. And gap years and technology are no longer just the province of teenagers, but big business for the baby-boomer market.

Maybe not so surprising when you consider that one in ten grandparents is under 50 and half of all the UK's 14 million grandparents are under 65. Indeed the majority (62 per cent) are no longer the senior generation in their family. Small wonder then that many grandparents are experiencing a whole new phase of life that has never existed before. They are healthy, busy (sometimes too busy) and as likely to tweet as to knit.

Middle age has spread – and the assumption that grans (health permitting) can't enjoy life to the full is perhaps not one to voice out loud (unless, of course, you have a death wish).

> 'I blog, I tweet, I travel, I go to the gym and out to eat. I like to dress well. I also get *very* peeved with anyone who tries to fob me off with bingo and Crimplene just because I've hit my sixties.' **(FeeTee)**

Gransnetters have made it clear (*very* clear) that whatever their actual age, very few grans consider themselves old.

> 'I'm not old, I am eighteen with forty-seven years' experience.' **(harrigran)**

In fact, old, the consensus suggests, is 10 years older than you are now. And these days many of those who've reached retirement age see themselves not as being at the end of an era – but at the start of a new, exciting period of their lives.

> 'I heard a saying on Radio 4: "You don't stop being young because you have grown old – you grow old when you stop being young." I feel better at 71 than I did at 50 ...

> The only thing that reminds me of my age is when my grandchildren seem to think I can't appreciate raunchy jokes – I haven't become less broad-minded with age.' (greatnan)

So what better time to launch *The New Granny's Survival Guide*? A book that takes grandparenting away from the blue rinse and brings it firmly into the 21st century with Gransnet's unique mix of ideas, information, practical support and, above all, our trademark sense of humour, wit and panache.

That's the thing about Gransnet: we've got grans. Tens of thousands of them in fact. They are warm. They are witty. They are (mostly) wise ...

In fact we've worked out that, between them, gransnetters have 326,741* years' experience in bringing up children, so they have had plenty of time to learn from their mistakes and accrue a fair bit of know-how along the way.

So mix all that with top tips, great writing and practical guidance and there you have it ... *The New Granny's Survival Guide*, the grandparenting book for modern grannies.

---

* Approximately

HOW THIS BOOK CAN HELP

Being a grandparent can be tricky at times. After all, parenting is one thing, but grandparenting comes with another generation playing piggy in the middle. They may or may not share your views, but they will certainly add another dimension.

Grandparenting is also changing, and we reflect that. The recession has piled even more pressure on working parents and their reliance on grandparents for childcare continues to grow.

A third of parents want to live closer to grandparents to take advantage of free (or cheap) childcare. Almost half of children under 10 with working mums are looked after by grandparents. Around a third of grandparents provide financial support for their children and grandchildren.

And with people living longer than ever before, it's hardly surprising that many grandparents now find themselves part of a new 'stretched middle' or 'sandwich generation', with not only children and grandchildren to help, but elderly parents to care for too.

'The media love to suggest that baby boomers are a bunch of self-indulgent, self-satisfied, selfish, rich dilettantes with an overinflated sense of entitlement and an endless succession of exotic holidays, during which they spend their kids' inheritance. They like to suggest that an intergenerational war is virtually inevitable and imminent.

'Maybe some grandparents are like this, but you only have to look at Gransnet to discover how false this picture is. Parents helping their adult children out financially with loans, gifts and house deposits – often jeopardising their own financial security in retirement; grandparents helping out with childcare, sometimes to the detriment of their own health; and loving relationships between three generations (or more) don't make good stories in the media.' **(absentgrana)**

The reality of grandparenting in the 21st century is that it's become a different kind of role, which throws up new questions. This is one of the many reasons why Gransnet has become so popular so quickly.

This book isn't simply the thoughts or advice of one grandparent but is backed up by the experience of thousands of grandparents from all over the UK and beyond. It's the collective wisdom of grans, on topics debated and explored on a daily basis, with questions coming up and being discussed minute by minute, 24/7.

This is our distillation of that amazing activity. Wisdom for all occasions in one handy book.

ABOUT GRANSNET

'You have to admit you have a problem to face up to your addiction – so, no, I don't have a problem spending 23½ hours a day on Gransnet.' **(glassortwo)**

Gransnet is the site for Britain's 14 million grandparents, as well as many others all over the world. Our users come from as far afield as Australia and New Zealand.

Launched in May 2011 as the big sister (mum/aunt?) to Mumsnet and described by *The Daily Telegraph* as 'a new dawn in grey power', we established ourselves from the beginning as *the* go-to site for grandparents.

Our forums cover everything from politics to sex, childhood games to difficult daughters-in-law. There are also recipes, product reviews and tips on everything from good grannying to great reads, as well as regular webchats with politicians, experts, authors and celebrities.

We also run forums for *The Oldie* magazine and Age UK and have helped members through bereavement, family breakdown and separation from grandchildren.

'It is so refreshing to know that others have the same problems/feelings/worries/happiness, etc. that one has ... whether it be worries about money/grandchildren/relationships/personal space/feelings/bereavement, etc. I could go on forever.' **(bikergran)**

CHAPTER ONE
BECOMING A GRAN

'I've said (sort of jokingly) that when you're a grandmother you have the best of all worlds, and, frankly, I'd have bypassed being a parent and gone straight to being a grandparent.' (everso)

HOW TO BE A GOOD GRAN-IN-WAITING

If the pregnancy seems to have gone by at the pace of a (very slow) snail, then the last couple of weeks of waiting for your grandchild to arrive can feel like an absolute eternity.

'I can well remember how anxious the wait was. Each hour seemed like a day and we were so on edge all the time. But when the baby did arrive the joy more than made up for the anxiety.' (littlemo)

Good things to do include: channelling your nervous energy into practical pursuits. Making a cot quilt. Knitting hats, booties and cardies. Baking ('Can't go wrong with a cake' has always been our motto). Filling the freezer with shepherd's pie (and cake ...).

Things to avoid include: watching back-to-back episodes of *One Born Every Minute*. Calling the parents-to-be every five minutes asking for news (even though it's the most tempting thing in the world). When there is something to know, you'll know – and, irritating though it may be, the fact remains that no amount of asking has ever hurried a baby into the world before they are good and ready (trust us, we've tried).

Try to enjoy the build-up. Not least because you may find that when the big day comes and things do get underway the waiting game gets even harder! Indeed many grans have told us they found the whole thing more nerve-wracking than when they were giving birth themselves.

'Partly because this time I had both my daughter AND the baby to worry about. And mainly because when I had her I was there (obviously!) so I knew what was going on the whole time ... pacing up and down, wearing a hole in the hall carpet, I could only imagine what was happening and that was so much harder.' (minette)

That said, don't turn up at the hospital saying what a terrible day you've had, worrying and waiting. Their day has almost certainly been at a different level of drama.

HAPPY BIRTH-DAY

And so the big day finally arrives.

It would be fair to say that giving birth has changed a fair bit over the last half-century. The technology has developed – gas and air has been around since the 1950s, but not all of us were able to take advantage of full-on epidurals – and the fashions in 'good births' have shifted accordingly.

For every new mother determined to take advantage of the all-pain-relieving drugs and machinery the NHS can muster, there will be someone else hoping to give birth like her great-grandmother, au naturel and keeping well away from doctors, perhaps assisted by the local wise woman (except these days they're called doulas).

Our generation might (or might not) have had an ultrasound (and possibly even found a surprise twin or triplet as a result); nowadays we can look forward to 4D scans showing the baby in perfect detail. It wasn't so long ago that dads were expected to pace outside the ward or go down the pub during the hard bit. Now if they're not working as hard as the mum ('Pass me that sponge', 'Where's my ice cube to suck?' 'Can't *you* have this bloody baby?') they're thought to be letting the side down badly. In what seems like a very short space of time, the maternity suite has gone from enemas and shaving 'down below' to the freedom of birth pools and birthing balls.

Hands up if *you* were advised to bring lip balm, CDs and a cooling water spray for the face when you gave birth?

If you were, you were clearly a thoroughly modern mother. But such things are now regarded as absolutely essential, along with a birth plan – where the parents-to-be might detail everything from their choice of pain relief to what music should be playing and what brand of scented candles should be strewn artfully round the room. It's probably best not to mention that the parents will reach a point where they couldn't give a stuff about the music.

WHAT TO DO IF YOU'RE THERE FOR THE BIRTH

> 'I cannot imagine my daughter allowing me anywhere near the sight of her down-there bits. Must be interesting though. I always felt I missed out a bit at my births, being at the wrong end.' (jangly)

'Down-there bits' on display or not, for some women it's important to have Mum there as an additional support in the labour room.

If your daughter or daughter–in-law has asked you to be present at the birth, do make sure that you talk through in advance exactly what she wants your role to be. Be warned though that what she *says* and what actually happens may be two very different things: we have known birth partners *to be bitten.* Still, sometimes when you are giving birth, you do need someone to bite.

If you are there as an extra person to offer reassurance, then allow her husband/partner to be her first source of encouragement. Resist the temptation to try to 'make it all better', however hard it is (and, oh, it is) to see someone you love in pain.

Your emotions may well be all over the place, but do try to stay composed (at least outwardly). Composure will have a calming effect on the labouring mum – in a way that running around shouting, 'Don't panic, Captain Mainwaring' probably won't – and will also conserve your energy for helping out afterwards.

NEWS OF THE NEWBORN'S ARRIVAL

Long gone are the days when the only way to hear about a birth was a call from the hospital payphone. Now new parents are as likely to text, tweet or post news of their new arrival on Facebook as they are to pick up the phone.

'I'm upset as we heard about birth by text rather than a call and also discovered they had announced it on Facebook many hours before bothering to phone the great-grandma – who was among the last to know.' (jojo)

If it really means a lot to you to get a call rather than a text, then say so beforehand (when there's something they can do about it) and not after (when it's a fait accompli and moaning about it will probably stir up bad feeling).

It's natural to expect grandparents to be top of the pecking order when it comes to hearing about a brand-new baby (and, yes – you have every right to feel a bit put out if you discover that there are photos on Facebook before you've even heard of the baby's arrival). But, if it's been a long labour, a difficult birth or a night without sleep, a text can be the quick and easy option. Plus – unlike a phone call – it will get to both sets of grandparents at the same time, which saves an awful lot of aggro over who got told the good news first.

GETTING TO KNOW YOUR GRANDCHILD

'I now have a beautiful granddaughter who is four days old. My son-in-law has two weeks off work and is very capable so I am not needed from a practical point of view. So how often do I visit? I don't want

> to be a nuisance by visiting too much but don't want them to think I don't care if I don't go enough. It goes without saying that I would move in if I could!' (newgranlin)

There is nothing lovelier and more adorable than a new grandchild – and no temptation greater than wanting to spend as much time with him or her as you possibly can.

Your support may well be needed every bit as much as the new family need their alone time, but it can be hard to strike a balance. So how much is too much when it comes to visits from Gran?

It's normal to want to spend every waking minute with the baby. Be upfront rather than trying to second-guess how best to fit in with the new parents' plans. This is a time when honesty really is the best policy.

Let them know that you think your new grandchild is the most wonderful thing on this earth and you'd like to spend 24/7 with them but clearly you appreciate that this isn't terribly practical (for them as much as you – because you're thoughtful like that).

Why not say that you remember this stage well? Tell them that while it was wonderful to have bonding time together as a new family you really appreciated help with cleaning, cooking and washing – so you're more than happy to do the same for them. Odds on they'll be flattered that you're putting their feelings ahead of your own.

> 'As a young mum what I would say is, be respectful of the parents and the fact that they need time to cherish the arrival of their little one. Offer help around the house and to your daughter as much as you can and bite your lip a lot!' **(hairfullofsnakes)**

Where you're based will also make a difference when it comes to visiting; clearly distance can be the decider. If you live far away, can you go and stay to help out? If you live close by, are you happy for them to ring at the last minute to fit a quick visit round wherever they've got to with the day? The more flexible you can be, the more likely you'll be able to drop by for another quick cuddle whenever the opportunity arises.

THE BABYMOON

This is a relatively new invention. You may have caught the start of the babymoon fashion, depending on when you last gave birth. Or, if you fell into the Dr Spock generation, it might be something you've never heard of.

Confusingly, the term can mean two completely different things. To some, it's a last holiday before the baby arrives (perhaps an abbreviation of 'baby-will-never-let-us-sleep-again-so-let's-lie-on-a-beach-and-relax-and-pretend-we're-on-honeymoon-before-we-spend-the-next-20-years-up-to-our-eyes-in-armbands-and-expensive-babysitters').

More often though, it's the name given to the bonding period for the new family – a chance for the couple to adjust to their new lifestyle (rather like the old-fashioned sense of a honeymoon, when couples had to get used to sleeping together, though this is more to get used to *not* sleeping) and to get to know their baby.

For many new parents, having Granny and the rest of the family along for the ride is part and parcel of the whole event. But other couples want to snuggle down around their new baby and be by themselves, revelling in the novelty of being a family. It's a natural enough thing to do, but can be (unintentionally) hurtful to an enthusiastic new gran.

> 'Son and daughter-in-law have indicated they want a week to bond on their own and get into a routine. I knew they didn't want lots of visitors straight after the birth but didn't dream this meant grandparents too.'
> (jojo)

This can and does happen. But, if you've had no warning, it can be a bitter blow and impossible to understand. Try to remember the feeling of being exhausted by the birth and overwhelmed by new responsibilities while batting off a surfeit of post-birth hormones. New parents can be frazzled and tearful, and they have to cope in whatever way they can. Visitors, even well-meaning grandparents, can sometimes be too demanding and tiring.

Don't sit and sulk. A small gripe can become a large grouch, and this is the time more than any other when relations need to be kept up.

And don't overwhelm or bombard them, although it's fine to send a text saying you hope that all is going well and that the baby is doing well and asking if there's anything they need.

However hard it feels, however long this short period seems to last, remember that if the baby is well and the parents are well then you will have many years ahead to enjoy being a gran.

> 'A few days now make very little difference. Let them bond as a family – there will be plenty of time for you soon.' **(butternut)**

Having a baby – particularly the first – is huge, life-changing and overwhelming, and it can take new parents (especially tired, hormonal and shell-shocked new parents) a little time before they feel ready to let the rest of the world in. But good things do come to those who wait.

> 'Believe me, when the new mum and dad are gagging for sleep you will not be on the sidelines then – they will be snatching your hand off to babysit.' **(glts)**

A HELPING HAND

Even if you're not needed at the beginning (or they think you're not), make sure they know that they only have to pick up the phone if you are able to offer help as soon as they need it. Ask what would make their lives easier. Let them know that when they are exhausted and just want to sleep you are happy to step in.

> 'Having someone to put the kettle on or rustle up a meal, etc. is usually pretty welcome. (Payment in cuddles of course!)' (rosiemus)

Visits are often doubly appreciated when the new dad goes back to work. It can be a daunting time for a first-time mum and knowing there's someone there to lend a hand is often appreciated. Just don't try to take over.

> 'Ask them what they need – one of the best jobs my own mum did for me was to pop around in the early days at an arranged time just to be there while I either had an hour's snooze or a bath, etc.' (hildaW)

If you can face it, why not offer to do the odd night shift during those early weeks? Even if the baby is being breastfed, it can be a huge help to a new mum to feed then hand over the baby so she can sleep while you change the nappy, wind, comfort or anything else that might be required.

PUT THE NEW PARENTS' FEELINGS FIRST

New mothers plus hormones flying round left, right and centre plus milk coming in (aka Dolly Parton day) generally equals a fair few tears (not just from the baby) and the odd cross word. But the good news is that these will generally be forgotten within a day or two.

Rack up brownie points for the future by putting their feelings first. Take your lead from the new mum and you won't go too far wrong. Remember that new dads may feel elbowed out by overenthusiastic (and far-more-experienced-than-they-are) grannies. And, tempting though it may be (and, oh, it is), do not ever, ever say 'I told you so'.

HOW MUCH ADVICE SHOULD YOU GIVE TO THE NEW PARENTS?

> 'Somewhere between none and none, in my experience. My favoured way is to listen to what she wants to do and say what a good idea that is.'
> (gracesmum)

Trying to be tactful can be one of the toughest parts of being a gran – particularly if you've been asked for your advice but they don't like your answer.

A useful rule of thumb is not to go against their style of parenting, even if it's one you don't agree with yourself.

Try to help them find a solution that may work within the framework they have set.

Try not to be critical and remember that parents know their own children better than anyone. Perhaps add, 'This is just my idea. You must do what you think is best and I will always support you in that.'

Talking about the problem can help without you having to offer an opinion at all – it's a classic counselling device. Ask what their options are; what they feel most comfortable with doing. What has the doctor/midwife/health visitor said? What would they like to happen?

> 'I don't give advice, even when someone asks for it. I just let them talk about the issue or problem and at the end they go away convinced I have provided the answer to their difficulty.' **(absentgrana)**

You might be itching to point out that, while they may well have read every parenting manual on the planet, the baby hasn't. Instead, try praising the positives and telling them that they're doing a grand job – it will mean the world to them. And if you do have pearls of wisdom you just can't wait to impart, do so – but make sure you choose your moment.

> 'I do hope as a grandmother I have the opportunity to give just two tiny bits of advice. (1) As long as you love your children and they know it, you can get away

with just about everything. And (2) For your own sanity, remember that YOU are in charge – you are a parent, not an entertainment director; create sensible boundaries and stick to them.' (joan)

SURVIVING THE TRANSITION FROM PARENT TO GRANDPARENT

Being a parent with full-on responsibility is different to being a grandparent (most grandparents, anyway – there are a few of us with full-on responsibility, but more of that later, see Chapter Four). The grandchildren may well be the centre of your universe, but it's an uneven relationship: if things are going well, you are not quite the centre of theirs.

There are definitely benefits to being part of the older generation (this time you get the good bits *and* a full night's sleep), but at times your role can be a bit uncertain. When you're the parent, everything is automatically your responsibility. When you're the grandparent, it's much more of a negotiation.

Drawing on your own experiences can be useful. If your own mother/mother-in-law was a perfect role model, then it's likely you'll want to try to follow her example. If not ... well at least then you'll know what *not* to do.

'I am about to become a grandmother for the first time. I'm really excited about it. I know we have to tread carefully. My daughter-in-law is super, but I still have memories of my mother-in-law's interferences when my first son was born. History will not repeat itself.' **(pengran)**

MOTHER KNOWS BEST

Trouble is – which mother? The one who's seen it all before ('But, Mum, times have changed!') or the brand-new one who's had her nose in Gina Ford/Penelope Leach/*What to Expect* since the second she conceived?

It can be difficult to adapt to the fact that so many things seem to have changed nowadays – and that often in the eyes of our daughters/daughters-in-law our many years of experience count for nothing.

'We are the ignorant generation. But we still love them, and adore their offspring. Don't we?' **(jeni)**

Research and medical advances have come a way since your own children were small and it can be hard to keep up with the fads and fashions that surround new babies.

No doubt you will have seen fashions come and go and parenting advice change, perhaps to become the opposite of what it used to be. For example, if you had a baby 30 years ago, the chances are you were encouraged to eat liver for the iron. Women having a baby now are advised not to eat liver *on any account.*

Gripe water is in. Gripe water is out. Dummies are de rigueur. Dummies are the devil's work. Newborns should wear gloves to stop them scratching. Newborns should no sooner be done up with gloves than sent to the moon. Newborns should be sent to the moon ... No, we made that last one up.

Some of these advances are fashions; some are real, honest-to-goodness actual advances. On the whole, it's best to go with the modern flow – mainly because you're going to have fewer arguments that way, but also because, well, not everything we used to do was perfect (hard as it is to believe). You will very soon learn that Google is your friend ... And Gransnet ...

Brush up on the current basics, but there will be times when your knowledge and experience will come in handy.

> 'What are the words to the "Teddy Bears' Picnic"? "Page the oracle ... Grandma!" We were walking last weekend and I was telling them the names of wild flowers. I was asked if I had a song about violets ... and I did.' (GrandmaLyn)

Here, to keep up your sleeve, is some useful information on how the land currently lies with some things that could just lead to a heated debate.

Swaddling

A tricky one. Swaddling, like so many of these things, drifts in and out of fashion and is currently very 'in'. District nurses might well have suggested it 40 years ago and hospitals are likely to do the same today.

And if this is the route the new parents have decided to take, it's likely whatever you say will fall on deaf ears.

Many tiny babies do feel more secure when tightly wrapped – and sleep better as a result. New studies into the safety of swaddling are still underway, but recent research suggests that parents should be cautious and ensure that babies won't overheat by keeping their heads uncovered and using only thin materials (such as a large muslin) as the swaddling blanket.

> 'My daughters-in-law perceived swaddling as verging on the barbaric so I never got to repeat the experience with my grandchildren. They also torched my suggestion that their babies should be put outside in the pram for their daytime naps, on the grounds that the babies may feel abandoned. So I quietly crawled back into my shell and just smiled in a granny kind of way.' (specki4eyes)

Cot Bumpers

You might have found the most perfect cot bumper for your grandchildren's visits – only to be told firmly that it's not to go anywhere near them.

Or you might be horrified at the very thought of the things and panicking because the new parents are insisting that it's the perfect final touch for the new baby's room.

Yes – they do look pretty. And yes – they are softer for little heads to bump into than wooden bars. But are the dangers of possible overheating and suffocation a myth?

It's hard enough when it's your own baby you're worrying about – when it's a grandchild it's trickier still to make your point without sounding like you are interfering or trying to show that you know better than the new parents.

So, once again, it's best to stick to the facts and the latest research.

In the United States a report from the American Academy of Pediatrics (November 2011) warned that cot bumpers were a known risk factor for cot death and that babies can suffocate against or be trapped by them. It also said that babies can be strangled by the ties that attach the bumpers to the rails of the cot.

In the UK The Lullaby Trust (formerly the Foundation for the Study of Infant Deaths) says:

> In the past, there were concerns that bumpers might make babies too hot, increasing the risk of sudden infant death. However, research has shown that they have neither good nor bad effects.

Take it out when your baby starts to roll. Make sure there are no trailing strings or ties.

Sleeping Position

As we've noted, many of the shibboleths surrounding small babies are little more than trends (albeit trends that anxious new mothers or perhaps even seen-it-all grans cling to rather aggressively). But sometimes research does prove that doing things differently can make a massive difference to the safety of a small baby.

About 30 years ago, babies had to be put to sleep on their fronts. A few years later it was on their sides, with a blanket tucked behind them to stop them rolling on to their backs.

But cases of sudden infant death have been significantly reduced in recent years and medical research shows that babies should now:

- be put on their backs to sleep, in the same room as the parents for the first six months
- be placed 'feet to foot' at the bottom of the cot so that they can't wriggle down under blankets and overheat
- have their heads uncovered and not be allowed to get too hot.

If you put your own children to sleep on their tummies in the belief that they are more likely to choke on their backs, this can be a bit of an adjustment.

'I think as grandparents it is up to us to stand back and watch what the mums have been advised to do, and then look at the research and learn about it and ask questions. We should only interfere if we are sure something is wrong. We must accept change (or progress, as I see it), as our parents had to with us. I hated it when my mother and mother-in-law used to say the dreaded words: "In my day ..." If things didn't change, we would all be still going down to the well to collect the water and carrying our babies on our backs – oh, yes, that is called "baby wearing" nowadays and is in fashion again!' (nanapug)

Equipment

Equipment is another thing that has come a long way since your own children were babies. There's so much stuff on the market now that it can be tricky to know what's really needed (not that much) and what's simply there to make life a little easier or more fun (most of it).

Add to that the fact that you need a degree in engineering to put some of it together (and, yes – some prams even come with assembly-instruction DVDs) and it's easy to get bamboozled. But, rest assured, you will not be alone.

'Most embarrassing moment when out for a walk with grandson: he went to sleep sitting bolt upright looking most uncomfortable with head lolling about and after about five minutes of struggling, we had to ask passing strangers with the same model of pushchair to show us how to lie him back.' (Jenjax)

Breastfeeding

This is yet another thing that seems to go in and out of fashion, and your views may well be influenced by what was the done thing when your own children were small.

These days new mums are actively encouraged to breastfeed. They may, of course, choose not to, or be unable to, but the majority (81 per cent at birth in the UK) do it at least for a while.

'If I am out and about, I do not want to be part of an act that should be private and quiet and personal! If I want to see bosoms, I can open a porn magazine, or page three of a newspaper – I do not want them at lunch.' (nanban)

'I love seeing women breastfeed and feel quite militant about women being allowed to feed their babies wherever they want. I can still remember being sent to the toilets of a famous London department store, even though I was sitting discreetly in a corner with a muslin over my front and no one could see any actual <shock-horror> breast. The toilets were incredibly smelly and unpleasant.' (getmehrt)

Nowadays breastfeeding is seen (by the majority) as normal and natural – and considered acceptable in many, if not most, public places. It might not be your thing, but if your daughter/daughter-in-law decides to do it, it's probably not wise to say you think it's a bit peculiar at the tea table.

Some men – particularly older men – do get embarrassed by it, but, dare we say it, they don't *have to look*. And most people would choose to celebrate the fact that we have moved on from an era where women were expected to lurk in the Ladies to feed their children.

> 'People who think breastfeeding is to always be done in "private" need to get over themselves. They don't have to look or stare at someone breastfeeding any more than they should stare at someone just sat nearby drinking coffee!' (maxgran)

Aside from anything else, it's now possible to feed so discreetly that most people wouldn't even notice a thing. There are special breastfeeding tops that save having to hoick bosoms out of the bottom of T-shirts and large muslins that can cover a multitude of flesh.

> 'And ... um ... isn't feeding babies the entire point of breasts in the first place?' (noodlenana)

'WE HAD IT SO EASY'

Once you see your children starting to bring up their own children, it's easy to think back to when they were small and make comparisons. But was it actually easier to be a parent 30 or 40 years ago than it is today? Were those of us who were children of the 1950s and 1960s, or our kids, a generation later, really more happy and disciplined? Or are the rose-tinted glasses simply making yesteryear seem like a better place to be?

There's no doubt that families these days are often far more child-centred than they were 40 or 50 years ago, when little ones were fitted in rather than fitted around. That said, those of us who were post-war babies were much more likely to have stay-at-home mums, at least in the early years. So the emphasis was different, but perhaps our parents could afford for it to be.

> 'You brought up your children more or less as your parents had brought you up. There were variations between one family and the next, but the broad agreement was that children should behave reasonably well, and not expect the world to revolve round their every whim.' **(elegran)**

Our generation of mums may have stayed at home or gone out to work, or a cobbled-together mixture of the two, but it is in the 21st century, when the minority of mums stay at home full-time, that parenting seems to have been turned into an art form.

Far more mums now work (whether through choice or necessity) and have to juggle jobs with parental responsibility and running a household. Yet expectations of them seem to be higher than ever before.

> 'I'd never been left with a baby before so I just got on with it with the occasional glance at Dr Spock and a large dose of intuition. These days you can't do this, you shouldn't do that, you can't feed them x, y or z or they'll get allergies/choke/hold it against you for the rest of their lives – because some "expert" says so. Well, mine seemed okay and have survived, despite dropping the odd one and leaving another in the car outside the post office and then walking home without her.' **(gally)**

It can be hard to get used to mums asking their children what they would like to wear, buy and have for tea, when you brought up your own to wear what you told them, eat what was put in front of them and you'd as soon have flown to the moon as ask them what they'd like to do for the day.

But, although times might have changed, children basically still need adults to behave like adults and take care of the big things.

'If they choose between sausages and fish fingers, they get practice at weighing up pros and cons without disrupting everyone else's day. If they have the universe to pick their tea from, they get lost, or become a nursery despot.' (Elegran)

GRANDPARENTAL RESPONSIBILITY

'I just worry so much, especially in the wee small hours – did I wash his hands sufficiently after our trip to the park and swings before lunch? Did I give him too much Calpol at bedtime? Worry worry worry! I would love to be a serene granny, taking it all in my stride and I do have all the patience in the world for him, but I could not live with myself if anything happened to him while in my care. I have absolutely no memory of worrying about our three daughters as they grew up, so am not a fussy mum – just a neurotic gran!' (gracesmum)

They might not be your responsibility full-time, but when it comes to looking after precious grandchildren it can be hard to resist the temptation to wrap them up in cotton wool to keep them safe. Even if you were happy to let your own kids run wild (and they turned out all right), letting go of this new generation of little ones can be surprisingly difficult. But the good thing is you won't be the only one to feel this way.

'There is something about being a granny that just makes you feel scared of having that much responsibility, and I never felt like that with my children. But, having said that, they are such a joy, and I'm not sure I felt that all the time with my own children!' (GoldenGran)

FEELING THE LOVE

The love you will have for your grandchildren may well be different from the love you feel for your children – but chances are it will be no less intense.

You may worry occasionally about them coming to harm, but at least you don't have to make decisions about where to send them to school or when they need a haircut or a new pair of shoes; you can just enjoy their company. You can spoil them (isn't that a grandmother's job?) as long as you know which rules are allowed to be broken from time to time. And you may find you have far more patience than when your own children were small and can give them undivided attention in a way that's just not possible when you're bringing up a young family yourself. Just a few of the many great things about being a gran!

'I did wonder if I would love any grandchildren as much as I loved my children. Of course I do, I adore my granddaughter. No worries about a career, housing, schooling, etc. Just time spent together doing things a two-year-old loves to do. I've always said you relive your childhood through your children and their childhood through your grandchildren.' **(dorsetpennt)**

CHAPTER TWO
BEING A GRAN

'What do I like about being a gran? EVERYTHING! Even the exhaustion after a long day with them. They are a never-ending source of wonder to me and I love them all to bits.' (riclorian)

WHAT SHOULD YOUR GRANDCHILDREN CALL YOU?

Gran, Granny, Nan, Nanny, Nonna, Nana, Gangy, Grandma, Gumpy, Guk (yes, really), Gorki ... there are no rules for what you should be called when you become a grandmother.

For some, the word 'granny' is like music to their ears. For others, it's rather more discordant:

> 'It's so ... grey hair and rocking chair. I'm just not ready to see myself like that.' **(rosiemus)**

You might want to pick the name that you used for your own grandmother. Or you may have one ~~foisted upon you~~ *carefully chosen* for you by your children.

Being able to smile sweetly and go with the flow will certainly make life easier (even if it does require the skills of an Oscar-winning actress) – but it's not for everyone:

> 'There was not a cat in hell's chance I was going to let them call me "Nanny". I am neither a goat nor someone who is paid to look after someone else's children, thank you very much ... Luckily we're all speaking again now.' **(kittyp)**

This, we've found, is an area where one man's (or, rather, woman's) meat is certainly another man's (woman's) poison. Some long to be called 'Grandma' from the second their sons or daughters find a partner (and long before they've reached the stage of actually making babies). For others, the word simply conjures up flashbacks of St Winifred's School Choir singing 'There's No One Quite Like Grandma' on *Top of the Pops* – all pink frocks, gappy teeth and hand-knitted cardies – and sends them running for the hills. Likewise, 'Granny':

> 'Especially if yours, like mine, was wizened, wore Nora Batty lisle stockings, wrap-around pinnies and zip-up suede boots in all weathers.' (sook)

Although – actually – we're quite keen on a lisle stocking ... but we digress.

Whatever your preference, the basic truth is that small children often have their own ideas. Indeed, we've come across a 'Gaga' (though she was only too keen to explain this was not as in 'dotty' – or 'Lady'), a 'Gram' (just because) and even a 'Giggle'.

What they can actually pronounce may well be the deciding factor:

> 'My mum wanted to be called "Nanna" but my eldest son could only manage "Anna", so it stuck and now all her grandchildren call her Anna – which is confusing for people who don't know, as her name is Alice, but her nickname is Babs. It's no wonder she's confused now ...' (Kittylester)

WHAT ABOUT THE 'OTHER' GRANDMOTHER?

When it comes to what you're called, it's worth bearing in mind that many new parents like to differentiate between paternal and maternal grandparents simply to avoid confusion. This can be a very simple process ('Granny

Ann' and 'Granny Alice' for example) or it can lead to handbags at dawn.

If you've set your heart on being 'Nan' (not 'Nanny') or 'Gran' (not 'Granny') it may be wise to get your towel down on the sunbed of pseudonyms early. If the other grandmother gets in first with the name you've fantasised about for years on end, then it can be hard to hide the resentment.

> 'I'd always set my heart on being "Nan", but my son-in-law's mother stole it from under me. She insisted it was what her other grandchildren already called her – though I'm convinced she simply coached them to spite me.' (FeeTee)

Just beware small children who choose to differentiate by observation. A great baker might well revel in the title 'Granny Cake', but the 'Nanny Gin' we came across was mortified. And 'Granny Squidge' wasn't quite sure whether to laugh, cry or lose a couple of stone.

NAMES IN DIFFERENT CULTURES

If your children (and grandchildren) live abroad, it may be worth noting any cultural references before selecting your sobriquet – witness the gran who plumped for 'Nana' only to discover on a visit to the family in France that she shared this name with a leading brand of sanitary protection ... and frankly might as well have called herself 'Always Ultra'.

We also came across a grandfather who was perfectly happy with 'Pop-pop' until his youngest grandchild informed him that this was the name most of her friends used for flatulence.

Perhaps it's simply wise to remember that a rose by any other name still smells as sweet – and once you see the beaming smiles the minute you walk into a room or feel those sticky little hands in yours you probably won't care what they call you anyway.

WHAT SHOULD/SHOULDN'T BE EXPECTED OF GRANDPARENTS?

It's easy to set the bar high (who doesn't want to be the perfect granny?) and we've all heard tales (quite possibly apocryphal – at least we hope so ...) of grandmothers who manage to hold down jobs while looking after grandchildren, cooking, ironing and cleaning for the family, not to mention babysitting and baking birthday cakes ...

We are the generation that invented juggling as a lifestyle, so it's slightly annoying to find that we're still expected to behave like circus performers:

> 'Surely our grandchildren will love us just as much if we are not would-be clones of their mummies? Are we trying to prove something?' **(gracesmum)**

Of course it's fine to be a supergran if you want to – if it's your choice rather than their expectation, and as long as doing their housework as well as your own, and generally being super-competent on everyone else's behalf, is not having an adverse effect on your own life.

It's more important, we think, for your children to know their little ones are being cared for by a doting granny than for them to worry whether you've turned their living room into a jungle camp-out. In our book, love and cuddles will always trump a tidy house (particularly when it's someone else's. Let them do their own hoovering!).

> 'My son's house tends to be chaotic but I wouldn't dream of trying to do any tidying. How they keep their house is none of my business unless it is indicative of other problems, which it isn't. Anyway it would be a waste of time: my son can untidy faster than anyone can tidy. The children are well loved and thriving. I give help when it's needed but have no desire to be any kid of "supergran" – I have a life of my own.' (FlicketyB)

SETTING UP A HOME FROM HOME FOR THE GRANDCHILDREN

If your grandchildren spend much time at your house, chances are you'll already have some of the paraphernalia they need. And it certainly helps visiting families to know they won't have to lug everything bar the kitchen sink whenever they come to stay – particularly if they're coming by train, plane or any other form of public transport.

So what do you really need to beg, borrow or ~~steal~~ *buy*?

If little ones are arriving late at night after a long journey, having somewhere to put them straight down will save a lot of aggravation, not to mention having to faff around with a travel cot in the dark (not something we've ever managed that successfully in the light).

A cot or cot bed is ideal, but if you don't have room to keep something up permanently, consider investing in your own travel cot. They last a surprisingly long time, can double up as a playpen for babies and can be stored under a bed or in a cupboard when not in use and put up when needed.

Other things that might come in handy are a highchair, changing mat, stair gate and nappies, as well as items like a digital thermometer and medicines suitable for small children (such as Calpol).

You don't have to spend a fortune. Borrow items from friends whose grandchildren are now older or try eBay, Gumtree, National Childbirth Trust (NCT) sales and charity shops, which can all be great sources of bargains. We're rather proud of the nifty sandpit we bought for a fiver in an online auction as it happens…

Do take particular care with car seats (a godsend to visiting parents arriving on public transport, as they are heavy and bulky to carry along with a small child, suitcase and the billion other things they seem to need for an overnight stay). It is essential that they have never been involved in an accident (which would compromise safety). It is definitely worth buying or borrowing from a trusted source.

Toys and books are also really useful to have as, again, they can be bulky or heavy to pack. The good thing is that they'll be used for years: we've found that what amuses a child at two can, oddly, amuse that same child at ten. Somehow the fact it's at Grandma's house makes it fun for a lot longer than it would at home. Digging out things that their parents enjoyed as children also goes down really well and adds to the fun (plus doesn't cost a bean).

What you need, of course, depends on how many grandchildren you have, how often they visit, how much you have room for, how much you mind your house being taken over and what you can afford.

> 'I do wish my children would remember I have a smaller house than they have and that sometimes I will be grumpy about all the paraphernalia left with me. My house is chock-full as it is, and every time I sit down to declutter I have to fight my way through all the stuff they have left with me over the years.'
> (Smyhouse)

Whatever you decide to have/not have, it's a good idea to consult your adult children before investing. Not only may they want to contribute financially to ensure that you have stuff they're happy with, but also this way there's no room for misunderstanding or worries that you are trying to take over. Oh, and tread carefully if you can afford things that the parents can't!

Some grandparents like to have a bedroom set up especially for their grandchildren. Of course for many this simply isn't possible, and, while it's lovely, it's absolutely not a necessity.

Whether you have a whole room set up or simply a small box of old toys, it's great for grandchildren to feel at home when they visit. How far you want your home taking over is entirely your call, although child-related detritus does seem to multiply alarmingly, whatever your intentions.

> 'Our dining room has been taken over by toys and my hope of having it solely as a dining room has long since gone to pot.' (goldengirl)

A word of warning for when they get a bit older: Lego pieces have a habit of being fatally attracted to the underside of bare feet.

FINANCIAL HELP

A question that is often asked is whether grandparents should finance their grandchildren – and indeed their grown-up children. Clearly your ability to do so is based not only on your inclination, but also your own financial position. If they need help and you can't afford to give it, then don't. But if you can, then where's the best place to start? And, equally, where should you draw the line?

You might want to help out with school or nursery fees. If there are after-school activities (drama, gymnastics, sports clubs, etc.) that the children would like to do but their parents can't afford, this may be a good place to start. It's easy to pass this contribution off as a birthday or Christmas gift if helping out financially is a touchy subject.

Some families make it a tradition for Granny to buy school shoes or uniform. Some grandparents choose to pass on their old cars instead of trading them in. Funding school meals or days out is a real boost to parents on a tight budget. Savings plans such as junior ISAs can be used later on to help with university fees.

Essentially, if you have disposable income while your family doesn't, then help is often welcome. If you don't, then do only what you can – it will still be appreciated.

'Pitch in where you are needed and wanted and at the level you can afford. In my case, daughter and son-in-law work hard and are proudly independent, but not that well off. So I'll offer to buy something useful and make a big play of it being a huge treat for me to spend some money on them. That way I can get away with spoiling the grandchildren, but on things they need. I think we are probably all fooling each other, but it's a system that works for us.' (HildaW)

HANDS-ON OR HANDS-OFF GRAN – WHICH IS BETTER?

'My daughter and I have one rule when we are together with my grandson and it's that she is his mum so she's in charge.' (babyjack)

Just one look at the many threads on this subject on Gransnet and you will see that these are very wise words indeed.

If you appreciated the help you got from your own mother/mother-in-law when your own babies were small, chances are you'll want to do the same for your children. But there is a very fine line between being helpful and too helpful, and treading it can be like crossing a minefield. Without a map.

Try to gauge what will keep the parents happy. Figure out what works for them as well as you. Tricky? Absolutely. But if you can get it right, it will make life an awful lot easier for everyone.

'I don't want to do the school run or drive myself potty trying to help out with this, that and the other. My daughters know I will step in at a moment's notice if there's a need, but I do things like cooking, playing, reading and outings as and when it suits me. I don't want to give all my time to my family. I love them all, but I want me-time and money and if that's selfish then so be it. I've worked hard and now it's their turn.' (Tanith)

It can be awkward to say no, even when it's hard for you to help. It's not always easy to watch your children do one thing with the wee ones when you really, really want to do another. And when you know you know best. But there is a rule here, and it's: the parents are always right, even when they're wrong.

Sometimes it really is tough to keep mum. But the golden rule is to try taking their lead rather than attempting to take over their parental duties. Taking a lot of deep breaths can help!

In short, ask before doing. Offer advice when you know it's wanted, not when you think it's needed. And remember that keeping the parents onside makes being a grandmother an awful lot easier – and a great deal more fun.

'It's a huge privilege to be a grandparent – and not a right. Being allowed to get to know my grandson is a complete joy and it's up to my daughter and her husband how and when I do that.' (HildaW)

SHOULD YOU MOVE TO LIVE NEAR YOUR GRANDCHILDREN?

How often you see your grandchildren will usually depend on how near to them you live. It's easy to idealise other cultures, where families live alongside each other, adorable babies sharing space with doting grans. We've all had that fantasy of baking cakes, dispensing wisdom, being revered by our children, adored by our grandchildren and, when the time comes, being looked after in our old age.

But in truth, these days Granny is just as likely to be far too busy for baking – plus avoiding carbs in any case – and living hundreds of miles away from her scattered family.

SHOULD I STAY OR SHOULD I GO?

'I'm torn between the places and people that I love at completely different ends of the country, and at the moment I'm spending too much time, money and emotion travelling between the two. And pleasing no one.' (quiltinggran)

The arrival of a new grandchild is one of those big life-changing events that can throw everything up in the air. It can make you question where you're living and why. If your home is hundreds of miles away from your grandchildren, you may well find yourself counting the days, weeks or months between visits.

But should you move? What if you've built up a social life and feel part of your local community? What if you know the best place to buy decent cake (important) and where to find the best plumber (not quite so important but still useful) and feel that you belong? The thought of having to start over somewhere new may well be utterly daunting.

You miss your family. And, although you don't want to be socially dependent on your children and starting from scratch is tough, you are still young and fit enough to make the move and meet new people. If you're going to go, then now would be the time, while you can still cope with upheaval, while there's time to make new friends.

You want to be close to your grandchildren, but you also like having somewhere for them to visit ...

Decisions, decisions. So what's the answer?

There are thousands of grandparents who find themselves in this position, agonising over leaving a home or life that's comfortable and familiar to be closer to the family they love so much. As one succinctly summed it up:

> 'This has to be the dilemma of our generation. I don't believe our parents' generation would have given it a moment's thought. When I was young I honestly believed life was settled and easy when you retired. Not true.' (megamutts)

Before calling the estate agents, it's worth considering the following questions:

- Can you afford to travel to see your children and grandchildren as often as you would like to?
- Are they prepared to come to you as often as you think they should?
- Do you agree about who is going to visit whom – whether you'll take it in turns or whether they will always come and see you? (Someone is going to be the guest and someone the host – and that may affect your relationship.)
- Do they have room for you to stay when you visit, or do you have to pay for accommodation in addition to travel costs?
- Do you *want* to stay in their house for a whole weekend? Would you rather be able to pop in for 20 minutes and scurry away again? Conversely, do you want all the work of entertaining them?
- If you are seriously thinking of moving, are you happy to leave your home and all its memories?

- When is the right time to move? Is it when you are able to get out and about and form a new social life? Or is it better to leave it until later, when your own independent life is narrowing and you are more focused on family?
- And, with the boot firmly on the other foot, if you need more help when you get older, how will that be for your children? If you move to be nearby, will you feel guilty for being a burden? And if you don't move, will you still feel guilty, because your family has to travel so far to visit and help out? (*Memo to self: stop feeling guilty about everything; they may actually want to help.*)

'When you are a relatively young grandparent the family might enjoy coming for weekend visits and holidays, but once the ravages of age set in, the trips to see Grandma can become a chore. That's what made us decide to sell up in order to be close to our family.' (PPP)

TOO CLOSE FOR COMFORT?

So you think you probably do want to move. But is there such a thing as being too near?

One survey shows that the optimum distance to live from your grandchildren is 28 miles (cue panic and search for very long tape measure...) and certainly a little distance can prove to be a good thing. Living very close may be great in theory, but sometimes a few miles can really make a difference.

> 'I've seen many friends whose families live very nearby end up feeling "put upon", as their children come to rely upon them as unpaid babysitters or emergency stopgaps.' (bakergran)

And then there's the issue of privacy. Much as they love you (obviously), your children and grandchildren might not want you to know about every little thing going on in their lives. And it works both ways. Do you really want them twitching the net curtains and keeping tabs on how many empty wine bottles you've left out for recycling? Without doubt this is something to think about if there are certain things you'd rather keep to yourself:

> 'I'm now dating again. But the thought of my daughter seeing a gentleman friend leaving in the wee small hours (and putting two and two together) fills me with horror. Although ... I'm sure as her mother I'm the one who's supposed to be disapproving of what she gets up to.' (Flibs)

THEY NEED ME MORE THAN I NEED THEM

Or do they? Your children may become reliant on you for help with the kids, but small children become big children in a scarily short time, as grans know because we've been through it all before. If you are basing your decision to move on making a new life around filling your time with looking after little ones, make sure you have thought about what happens when they don't need you quite so much any more.

Empty nest syndrome is no easier to bear the second time round – and may actually be harder if you are no longer in familiar surroundings or with work and friends close by.

And, given that resentments can flow both ways, it's worth being clear about what everyone expects before you pack up and move halfway across the country. Agree terms *before* making the move. Make it clear you are at liberty to say no to requests for backup childcare or babysitting that you can't do or don't want to do, however happy you may be to help out the rest of the time.

Outline rules about 'popping in'; they won't want you interrupting a dinner party any more than you want them bursting in while you're in your dressing gown and face cream, casually picking at a family-sized pack of Maltesers in front of the telly.

Establishing the ground rules from the outset means that frustrations and feelings of being taken for granted – on both sides – are less likely to creep in and spoil a close relationship. (And it is worth remembering that they may be worrying about all this every bit as much as you are.)

A positive plan is to make sure the benefits of being close by are shared. Perhaps while the children are small you can help with babysitting, looking after poorly babes while parents are at work, feeding the cat/dog/iguana while the family is on holiday. Then when you get older and, perhaps, need more practical support, they can be on hand to help you in return.

IT ALWAYS SEEMS SO LOVELY WHEN WE VISIT

And why wouldn't it? Holidays are always (or at least usually) golden time precisely because they are holidays – a break from home and all the everyday-life-ness that entails.

But how much do you really know about the location? Moving lock, stock and biscuit barrel is very different to a weekend visit. It pays to do your homework first, and it's worth finding out what's available in your current interest areas (and the ones you might like to develop), for example art classes, walking groups, book groups and voluntary work.

One tip we like: if can you spend time in local shops and cafes and get chatting, you will get a better feel as to whether it's a friendly spot or not.

And one tip we *really* like: remember to check that Majestic will deliver wherever you move to.

PERMANENT MOVE?

Not necessarily. If you're really not sure you're doing the right thing, how about considering a trial run? Try renting, rather than selling up and buying, to give yourself a temporary safety net.

> 'It's worked out well for most of my friends who've moved to be near their families. But one spent 18 months desperate to go "home" – and because she wasn't tied to a property she was able to do so.' (jakesgran)

Renting in a new area is often a good idea in any case. You get a feel for the place and can work out what shops, social amenities, transport, etc. you need to be near.

WHAT THE FUTURE MIGHT HOLD

If you're moving the length of the country to spend time with your grandchildren, the last thing you want to discover is that they're at after-school clubs every day and at parties/football/ballet/sleepovers all weekend, every weekend.

And are the family you are moving to be near committed to staying put long term?

> 'I am put off the idea of moving because I have known of several instances when the gran has moved to be near the family, who have then had to move elsewhere

because of a job change or promotion. The curse of social mobility!' (annobel)

Whatever happens longer term, if you throw yourself into a new place and become part of that community as well as involving yourself in your family, the chances are you'll be fine.

'We returned from France to a totally new place, have made new friends and have enjoyed being a BIG part of our daughter's and little grandson's life. Now they are thinking of moving to the States and we are devastated. If there is a chance that your family may move, you need to have friends around you so you are not left on your own again.' (AmberGold)

FITTING IN

This is essentially what it all boils down to. Do you find it easy to socialise? If the answer is yes, then getting out and meeting new people will be part of the fun. If the answer is no, you will have to make more deliberate plans to get out and about as soon as you move. Feeling isolated will make the transition an awful lot harder and the new arrangements a bigger adjustment for everyone.

'If you do move, the one thing to do is join everything. We moved back to my husband's hometown after 40 years. We have met so many people who have moved to our small town knowing nobody and the ones who settled down have been the people who go out and work in the charity shop, etc. I have a neighbour who lost her husband and is so isolated as they just spent time with each other. I can go shopping and take hours, as I meet so many people to speak to. She goes down town and knows nobody.' **(eleanorre)**

Moving to be closer to children and grandchildren is a big step, however keen you are to do it. But by throwing yourself into your new life, getting involved with the community as well as the family, taking up new hobbies and enjoying old ones, you might find you get a new lease of life into the bargain.

'Looking back, we were very much in a rut before and could easily have stayed there. This is the best thing we've ever done.' **(Zephrine)**

EENY MEENY...

What happens if you have more than one set of grandchildren in more than one place? If your children live at opposite ends of the country, are you going to put noses out of joint if you move close to one and not the other(s)?

> 'Bear in mind that they will feel simultaneously glad, guilty and envious that you have "chosen" another sibling over them to live with/near.' **(Twinklepickers)**

Make sure that all your children understand why you've chosen to make that particular move. Discuss what you will do to make sure that the ones living further away don't miss out. And, though it's often difficult to talk about up front, ensure that you've worked out together what happens in case of bereavement or needing care and how this responsibility might be split fairly and practically.

MOVING ON – OR MOVING IN?

> 'My friend's father moved into a flat next door to them and it worked out so well: he had his independence, but when he became less able they were able to help him out without it becoming a big chore for them.' **(Babyjack)**

There are many great things about multigenerational living and many, many things to pin down before you even think about agreeing to move in with your grown-up children and their family.

There are also plenty of ways of doing it: granny flats, converting garages or outbuildings, buying interconnecting properties or pooling resources to buy something together that you'd never be able to buy apart. And all – naturally – have their pros and cons.

The plusses of moving in together (or virtually together) include independence with the security of someone nearby if you need them, plus company and support. And having you there can be great for bigger grandchildren (who sometimes need a sympathetic ear) as well as little ones.

But there are plenty of things to think about before going ahead:

- Will you have your own front door? This can make a huge difference.
- Will you each pay your own bills – or a contribution to the household expenses as a whole?
- Will you cook and eat together? (Regularly? Always? Never?)
- What will happen if you need care in the future? Is your arrangement suited to doing this in situ? Or would you have to move out? (And, of course, how would that impact on the others and their plans for the future?)
- What would happen if they needed to move or downsize for some reason (divorce, redundancy, etc.)?

It's never pleasant to address the worst-case scenario, but it's usually wise.

STAYING PUT

Staying put doesn't have to be a bad thing.

> 'My mum never moved to be near any of us (I'm one of five) and it turned out just as well, really, because we all moved about quite a lot. Plus she has a good social network where she is and where we all grew up.' (baggy)

Of course, if your grandchildren live round the corner you're likely to see them a lot more than if they live in Sydney, but, wherever they live, how much you see them will depend on work, childcare arrangements, the relationship between you and their parents and all manner of other practical considerations.

However doting you might be, small children can be utterly (if deliciously) exhausting and you wouldn't be the first to be delighted when they arrive – and equally delighted when they go away again too.

> 'Mine live an hour and a quarter away – so I see them once a fortnight during term time – but they come and stay in the holidays, including half-terms. Actually I think that's about right for me. Love 'em to bits but I like my me-time these days.' (jangly)

If distance means you can't see them as much as you'd like to, don't forget that technology can at least help to bridge the gap. Some grandparents got their start with computers thanks to Skype. For families that are spread across different countries or even continents, online communications can bring the grandchildren into your house on a daily basis. A virtual visit may not be the same as the real thing, but it can be a pretty good stopgap.

> 'We see our grandson about once a month – he lives several hours' drive away. But we see him most days on Skype – and now he recognises us on the screen, which is great.' (pompa)

COPING WITH COMPETITIVE GRANNIES

There are times when being a good gran can seem like an Olympic sport, and 'granny wars' can be no less intense than any other battle (knitting needles at dawn?).

> 'Recently my daughter made some comment about how the other granny has much more "equipment" for the boys, in this case beakers, and I just felt the tears well up and said, "Please don't start granny wars, that is just unfair." She realised that what she had meant in jest had actually been hurtful, so I can admit to oversensitivity in the granny-comparison area!' (gracesmum)

It's true that it can be tough to survive the 'other' grandparents, although it's worth remembering that they are likely to be thinking the same and you're probably both doing an equally great job.

Likewise, dealing with friends' tales of 'perfect' and overachieving grandchildren is never easy. And, if you are careful not to regale friends and family with every detail of your own grandchildren's lives, it can be irksome in the extreme to spend time in the company of those who can talk about nothing else.

> 'Before my sister had a grandchild she thought I talked too much about mine. Then she too became a granny ... Think about it, though – when everything is so grim outside our own four walls, perhaps we need to talk about things or people that make us cheerful – and my grandchildren certainly do that for me.' **(annobel)**

It is hardly surprising that people are besotted (aren't we all?) and it can, of course, be lovely to share news and funny stories. But when someone has made it an art form and can find a way to bring discussions on the weather, politics, sport, work, even the state of your wardrobe back round to their wee ones, moving the conversation on without causing upset can be an uphill battle.

You can try smiling sweetly and letting it wash over you (while you plan what to make for dinner). You can subject them to 500 photos of your holiday on the Norfolk Broads to get your own back. You can parachute out of a plane so you can tell them all about it and leave them so gobsmacked that they can't utter a word (extreme, yes, but it does work).

Or you can start a conversation with something like:

> '"Let's have five minutes' worth of grandchildren news ... you tell me yours first and then I'll tell you about mine." Out come photos and we ooh and aah an awful lot. After which it's all hunky-dory because we've each had centre stage.' (supernana)

WHEN YOU'RE WORRIED

Being a gran is – for the most part and for most people – a joy and a pleasure. But, as with any relationship with people you care deeply about, there may be times when worries creep in.

For example, while we all know that children develop at different rates and at different times, sometimes it's hard not to be concerned when a grandchild isn't doing what, say, one of their siblings was doing at the same age. And when you're a grandparent it can be harder still to know when to say something and when to keep your concerns to yourself. It's perfectly normal to worry about the ones you love. What you do about it will depend very much on the circumstances.

Have the parents mentioned to you that they are worried? If they have, then discussing your own concerns may be easier. Offering support and practical ideas at the same time may help you all deal with the issue without needless panic. The wisdom of experience ('I remember worrying about the same thing when you were small, but look how it all came good in the end …') is helpful where appropriate. If it's a situation that's new to you all, it can still be a great comfort to the parents to know they are not alone and that they have someone else on side.

If you are worried about something but the parents haven't mentioned anything or don't seem concerned, that makes it rather more tricky.

If it's a developmental issue, it's worth researching the range of what's considered normal in this area. This can often cover a much broader age range than you might have expected and simply finding out more can help put your mind at rest. For example, if your child walked at 10 months and your grandchild is now 18 months and still rooted firmly on their backside, it can be easy to think there's a problem. But, in fact, both are perfectly normal. (If they're still not on the move six months later, it's a different matter.)

Ask yourself whether you need to get involved. If the parents are doing a good job with everything else, it's likely they'll have this covered too.

If it's a very small child still under the care of health visitors or other professionals and nothing has been mentioned, then it's fair to assume that they are either aware of the problem and monitoring it or don't think that there is anything to worry about at this stage. Likewise, if it's an older child at school, teachers are likely to mention anything of great concern.

> 'Our grandson didn't utter a word until he turned two – a very odd experience for us, as all four of our children had pretty good nattering skills by that age. I used to babble incessantly to him in the hope he would start to speak. One day I asked what he would like for lunch when I had my back to him – and he replied, "Chicken curry." Turned out he could speak, but couldn't actually be bothered as he could get whatever he needed by pointing at it.' **(Jams)**

Worrying about what's going on at the family home (if parents are divorcing, for example) and how it might be affecting your grandchildren is more difficult. Even if it's clear you have their best interests at heart, parents going through a tough time themselves may find what they consider 'interfering' as the final straw.

Of course this doesn't mean you should sit back and do nothing if you are genuinely concerned. With older children it can be easier: if you are spending time together in a safe and loving environment, they may well be able to voice any worries that they have and you can discuss what to do about them together. With smaller children this obviously won't be the case, but a supportive word to Mum or Dad ('I know you are having a really hard time at the moment and that you hate little Jimmy hearing you argue because it upsets him. Can I help at all?') can often make a difference.

It is definitely worth remembering that small children can be quirky in the extreme and something that might trigger alarm bells can have a perfectly innocent explanation.

> 'As a tiny child I liked art but would draw everything upside down – chickens, lamp posts, people – everything. Oh, and the people I drew were all starkers. Mum wanted me to see a child psychiatrist. Dad said I'd come right in the end. Dad was right. Ish.' (joan)

CHAPTER THREE
FAMILY

'I love nothing more than spending time with my wonderful family. Is it wrong that I also love the peace when they've all gone home again?' (northerngran)

FAMILY RELATIONSHIPS

You've had a lifetime to get used to your kids. You've done your best to give them the right values and ideas, and now you're watching them pair up and create families of their own. This means you've suddenly got a whole load more people to get to know and grow to love.

Sometimes (though fortunately not always) your children will pick partners you wouldn't have chosen for them in a million years. Partners who don't have the right job, the right opinions, any opinions at all ... in short, partners you can't quite see the point of.

So how best to welcome their choice of significant other into the family, especially if they're not the one you'd have picked for them yourself?

> 'I'm not sure one has to actually like them, though I'm sure it's very nice. It's their life and as long as the partners are keeping our sons and daughters happy and they are living the life they choose then it's up to us to be quietly supportive. That being said ... if one caused either of my girls any grief I would be at his throat!' (HildaW)

Of course if you actually like the people that your children have chosen as life partners and they turn out to be loving partners and parents and you all get along like a house on fire, then you're doing pretty well. But what happens if you don't always (ever?) see eye to eye?

First, ask yourself if their partner is making your daughter or son happy? Do they treat them well? Are they a good parent? If the answers are yes, then accept that you may never be best friends but they are giving your child the life you wanted for them and that, at least, is a result and something to be grateful for.

If you do have the odd (frequent?) reservation, be comforted by the knowledge that there are many others in the same boat. It's inevitable that the son-/daughter-in-law relationship – just like any other relationship – can have its ups and downs, and learning to take a deep breath and walk away from a row is a must.

Do remember that it can take time to get to know someone properly and to fully uncover the qualities that helped your own son or daughter fall in love with their other half in the first place.

> 'I adore them now, but truth be told I was very suspicious at first. Probably would have put them under surveillance if I'd had the finances.' **(lionlilac)**

You might not always agree or hold the same opinions – all perfectly normal – but if you are able to respect each other's point of view this will help provide a firm footing for the future. Just think ... without them, there wouldn't be those precious grandchildren in the first place. And they're definitely a gift worth learning to bite your tongue for.

> 'I'm very happy with both my son-in-law and my daughter-in-law. To me, I don't have in-laws, I have bonus children, whom I love like my own and who call me "Mum".' **(Swedenana)**

You too could be one of the lucky ones. You might find you like each other without having to make any effort at all and end up loving them like your own. Or even more ...

> 'I like my daughter's boyfriend so much I told her that if they split up I was keeping him out of the two of them.' (purpleandredhat)

One word of caution: however keen you are, it is possible to overinvest in other people's relationships. It's often said that you can't be certain what goes on inside anyone else's marriage and this is true even if you're talking about your own child.

> 'I like my son-in-law. I really liked my ex-son-in-law too, but as my other daughter said ... you didn't live with him! True!' (milliej)

WHAT IF YOU *REALLY* DON'T GET ON?

Needless to say, in an ideal world we would all do the 'love thy neighbour' bit and go around spreading goodwill and baking cakes for each other 24/7. (Ours is a lemon drizzle. Thank you.) But that's not the real world (which is good news at least for our waistlines). The sad truth is that there will always be some people who seem to have a knack of upsetting and hurting others, and there will always be some you simply can't get along with, no matter how hard you try.

Walking away from these disruptive types may be the best thing to do, but when they're married to one of your kids it all gets rather more complicated.

> 'We tried to like our ex-son-in-law as we respected our daughter's choice. The effort lasted about five minutes. In the couple of years that followed their marriage, we grew to loathe him heartily. We rejoiced when our daughter finally saw the light. But throughout the misery of her marriage we decided never to bad-mouth the guy, just be non-committal, because she was unhappy enough without our input.' **(amma)**

Putting your own feelings to one side is a wise move (unless, of course, your child or grandchildren may be at risk). If you do spot the signs that there might be a problem, by all means say your piece (tactfully!), but then, rather than retreating to your corner before the next bout, with boxing gloves still at the ready (tempting), work to keep the channels of communication open. This is particularly important if your son- or daughter-in-law is aware of your feelings, as they may try to sever contact with you to retain control. So support rather than criticise and be there when needed to pick up the pieces.

Of course it's never easy when your delight that your child has met someone they want to be with turns into sadness that the relationship is not working out as you hoped. Separation and divorce are never easy, but if their choice is to stay and try to make it work, even though it isn't making them happy, that can feel even worse. And then when babies come along it can muddy the waters further still.

Your children don't stop being your children just because they've grown up and got married or found a partner. But there does come a point when they are old enough to make their own decisions and you have to let them (*clamps lips together and digs nails into palms*).

All mums want their children to be happy. And if they are then, whether you approve of their partner or not, they're doing okay. Take comfort in that and accept that things are a lot better than they could be.

DIFFICULT DAUGHTERS-IN-LAW

> 'I think the old saying "A son is a son till he finds him a wife, a daughter's a daughter for the rest of your life" is so true. My mother-in-law was very nice when we were "courting", but as soon as we announced our engagement she went on the defensive. It took us until my son was born to get over our differences and we became the best of friends. I miss her so much since she has passed away; all I can say to all mothers-in-law and daughters-in-law is: learn to live with each other as individuals, and not enemies fighting for the son's attention. You might find your best friend.' (glassortwo)

The problems we've outlined above are often most acute when it comes to the relationships with daughters-in-law. Many women enjoy wonderful mother-/daughter-in-law relationships. Some have it from the start, some have to work at it, but there will, unhappily, always be some who never quite get there.

The reasons for this can vary hugely. Perhaps it's a struggle to feel that someone with very different ideas and background is really part of the family. Your daughter-in-law might be keen to suggest that the way she was brought up was better. And some mums can regard their relationship with their sons as so special that it's inconceivable to 'lose' them to another woman who will now be taking first priority in their lives.

> 'My mother-in-law was a wonderful woman and my best friend, and I certainly don't put that down to just me being friendly with her, but also her ability to open up her heart and her home to a woman who was about to take first place in her son's life. It takes two to tango but at the same time three doesn't have to be a crowd.'
> (lucyjordan)

No matter how hard you try, there will always be some daughters-in-law who remain resistant to your efforts to make them welcome and love them like your own.

> 'Mine is totally possessive with my son and doesn't like him to visit us for more than 45 minutes. She sees us as a threat, although none of us is. At the same time she spends full days with her family. I am learning to just enjoy visits if they happen, but it is a pity. She has

never confronted me but gives me evil looks when my son is not looking.' **(Bea)**

It's always easy to take a situation at face value, but sometimes it pays to dig a little deeper. Could you conceivably be imagining the evil glares? They may (of course) be very real, but, equally, she might be giving you a nice look which is just not translating well! She might be shy or awkward and only able to cope out of her own 'safe' environment for short periods of time.

Or there may indeed be an issue – even a misunderstanding – which is coming between you and will continue to jeopardise your relationship until something changes. If this is the case, tread carefully. Don't confront her to find out what's wrong, but perhaps initiate a casual conversation with your son. Tell him how much you enjoy their visits and (without putting any pressure on) how you do hope that they will be able to stay for longer sometimes. Ask whether your daughter-in-law feels comfortable with you/at your house and whether you can do anything to help her feel like it's a home from home, where she's welcome at any time.

Stay positive and calm (even though you may want to wail and drum your fists into the floor) and be reasonable. In short, make sure you don't come across as interfering, but as loving, concerned and welcoming.

If you can't get along, perhaps arrange time with just your son and grandchildren. (You never know ... your daughter-in-law may be so grateful for a bit of time to herself that it could make all the difference.)

If there's something you really disagree about, as long as it's not causing actual harm to anyone, try to respect her opinions. People need to learn from their own mistakes, much as we would like to be able to put them right (*we* know that grans know best, but sometimes you just have to keep that to yourself), and unfortunately the fallout from what can start as a small disagreement can quickly affect everything.

Relationships can spiral downwards if no one makes the effort to stop them from doing so. This can result in alienation from your children and grandchildren. There are occasions when biting your lip is the better option.

> 'Do you want to be right, or do you want to be happy? Sometimes you just have to decide between them.'
> (greatnan)

It might not be easy, but it's always worth trying to pull out all the stops. You both have the same person's best interests (your son's) at heart and it will certainly make life much happier for him if you can get along. Do your best and you will know that at least you have done the right thing.

Do make sure you stay on good terms with your son. You don't want him to have to take sides – it will only end in tears. It's probably not a fight you're going to win, and, put like that, why would you want to?

> 'Family life has to keep going, we all have to keep some of our opinions to ourselves. I remember an interview on BBC TV with a couple, both over 100. "What is the secret of a happy married life?" the reporter asked him. "Yes, dear!" he replied. So there we are, we mothers-in-law. A little bit more of "Yes, dear."' **(Expatmaggie)**

If you had a great relationship with your own mother-in-law, ask yourself what she might have done when things got a bit tricky. And if you didn't, well, at least you can use your experience to your advantage.

> 'Having had difficulties with both of my mothers-in-law, I've always been profoundly aware that one day it will be my turn to be the "Wicked Witch of the West" to my son's future partner ... When he was first born I actually used to say to him, "One day your wife is going to hate me." LOL.' **(nonna2)**

Was Janet Street-Porter right when she said that mothers always resent their son's partners? The evidence that we've found suggests she's actually very wrong. Getting to know someone new can take time. Introducing someone new into a close-knit family environment can take time. Learning to love someone can take time. But that's not to say it doesn't happen and that a happy ending isn't entirely possible.

> 'We are all only too naturally sympathetic to our children and don't get that they may not be as perfect as we think/hope. You and your daughter-in-law may both be very nice people who don't understand each other; she might be awful but you can overcome that for the sake of your son and grandchildren; you are a woman chock-a-block full of life's experiences and wisdom – a place she will arrive at one day, as we all know, but maybe not in your time!' **(Nanaban)**

Trying to include a daughter-in-law in the same way you would a daughter – if you have one – can certainly help her not to feel like an outsider in her new family, and also ensure that she doesn't see you as competition for your son's affections (even if you aren't and never have been).

> 'My avowed plan was to try very hard to love whoever my son fell in love with and married based on the theory that we both loved the same man.' **(Gagagran)**

DISAPPROVING OF THE WAY YOUR GRANDCHILDREN ARE BROUGHT UP

And we're back to buttoning that lip. (It's starting to ache a bit now, from all the buttoning, to be honest.)

When you don't agree with the way your grandchildren are being brought up, it's hard to know when – or if – to say something or whether speaking up at all will only make things worse.

Picking your battles is the best plan. If it's something you'd do differently but it's not doing anyone any harm (and, yes – you might have to take a big step back to admit this), then take a lot of deep breaths, throw a teacup or two by all means, rant to the cat, the budgie or even the postman – but when it comes to the parents, keep shtum.

If it's something that's going to have a knock-on effect for the grandchildren or that's affecting your relationship with them, then, yes, speak up. But tread carefully. Think minefield invaded by crocodiles with a sniper or two on the side ... even if the parents are equally concerned about what's gone wrong.

> 'I feel in a quandary about my grandson's behaviour – do I say what I think (which is that he does not get clear boundaries and they need to get their act together on this) or do I continue to try and bolster their confidence as parents and avoid anything that might be construed as criticism? I do not want to risk alienating them or causing any sort of rift, but on the other hand all the wider family are also concerned.' **(Mishap)**

A constructive approach is to start with the positives. Find things to compliment: if they are consistent with boundaries or they stand their ground when pushed; if they speak calmly even when they are really upset; tell them how much you admire their stance before adding your suggestions.

If you are looking after your grandchild and find certain behaviour unacceptable, tell the parents that when they were young this is what worked so well and you'd like to try the same, but obviously you would like to remain on the same page as them. You never know, they might secretly be grateful for some top parenting tips that you prototyped and tested out so successfully on them!

> 'I think phrasing advice as "some people would say that ..." and "I read somewhere the other day that if you ..." can help get advice across without sounding like you are telling them how to do it.' (mamie)

There are no hard and fast rules for dealing with children, and different children will react differently to discipline. What works perfectly with one may not with another. You may have more experience, but when things go wrong and the parents are present it's very hard to step in without them feeling undermined.

> 'When my grandson developed one or two "challenging" habits, I asked his mum if we could agree on a plan to deal with them, so that we had a consistent approach and were not giving him mixed messages. She had to

decide on the plan, but I had the opportunity to suggest one or two things gently. I also had a reason to give feedback on how the plan worked for me and what I tried instead if it didn't.' (nuttynorah)

But how does it work on occasions when Mum and Dad aren't around and Granny is in charge? If you're left in loco parentis, are you entitled to discipline as you see fit? Or should you always defer to the parents, even when you're doing them a favour?

'If they are in my house (or car), then the children have to abide by my rules and they have always accepted this. Middle granddaughter was a horrendous toddler and her mum would walk off and leave me with her, her excuse being she looks like me so everyone would think she was mine!' (janreb)

Certainly 'my house, my rules' is an approach adopted by many and it's perfectly fair, within reason, to expect anyone (child or adult) to behave in a way you feel is acceptable within your own four walls.

'My husband struggles with the concept of not imposing discipline on home turf and I've been known to take away toys or sweets if bad behaviour persists. But when we are at their house, my daughter has already asked us not to be involved in any discipline-

> related matters (even to back up her and her husband) as she says this is a parental not a grandparental matter.' (GrandmaAnge)

The last thing you want to do with small children is to confuse them by letting them think that something they are not allowed to do at home is absolutely fine when Mummy and Daddy aren't around. That's not to say the odd treat can't creep in here and there – but when it comes to discipline consistency is key.

Have the conversation beforehand and try to agree on boundaries and how to apply them. Some rules are meant to be broken, some really aren't. If they're not eating a certain food because of a food scare or dietary restrictions, it's not your business to countermand instructions (even if you think the parents are overreacting). However, if your grandchild is not supposed to have sweets except on Saturdays, a chocolate button on a Thursday isn't going to cause lifelong scarring.

If there is something you disagree on fundamentally, like how to deal with tantrums, make it clear that you are happy to look after your grandchild but only if you are able to keep things running smoothly, which means exercising a degree of authority. Children need to know that someone is in charge (and you may well find that they behave far better for Granny – and Grandpa – than they ever do for Mum and Dad).

Start as you mean to go on with discipline and have an idea what you're going to do if your original tactics don't work. The key thing is to keep calm. Ish ...

THE OTHER GRANDPARENTS

We touched on competitive grannies earlier, but is there actually a pecking order when it comes to being a gran? Does the maternal grandmother have more clout? Should you take a back seat if you're the paternal grandmother? What if one grandmother seems to be favoured over the other? What if the other grandmother can offer more than you can?

> 'I do think it's only natural that daughters tend to be closer to their own mothers, and sometimes there can be female rivalry (even if unadmitted) between the mother and the wife of a son. A lot depends on the individual relationships between the parties. Personalities can clash too.' (Anagram)

Chances are that if a woman is close to her mother before she has children, she'll be close to her mother after she has children as well (yes, yes, it's not rocket science). But that doesn't mean there's no room for anyone else – and if you're the mother of sons, please don't panic.

'My daughter's mother-in-law is a lovely woman. But when the first grandchild was born, she said, "I know I'll always be number two granny." I found this so sad and said, "No, we'll be first equal." My daughter really loves her (she has two sons and no daughters) – they have fun together and I think she appreciates the advice of an older woman who doesn't have the same emotional involvement with her as I do. It's about sharing – there's enough love for everyone.' **(Granmouse)**

A perceived hierarchy can be based on all sorts of factors, some of which have not the slightest thing to do with the other set of grandparents.

For example, how close by do you live? If one set of grandparents lives round the corner and the other, a four-hour drive away, it's almost inevitable that the ones who live nearby are going to end up being more hands-on. But does that mean they're going to come top in terms of love and affection? Absolutely not. You don't have to see your grandchildren every day to be close to them.

'I am closer to my daughter's boys, but that's because of the children they are. They live further away than my son, whose boys I find impossible.' **(ChristineH)**

The long and short of it is that every family is different and every set of relationships is different.

If one set of grandparents goes out to work and the other is retired, that may affect the balance. If one lot has similar interests and the others like completely different things, that can also have a bearing – regardless of whether you're maternal or paternal grandparents and whether all of you like, or love, each other or not.

> 'Try not to see this as a competitive event – it will only spoil the joy of being a grandma. Just fit in where it's needed, let it happen naturally and see each occasion that you are involved with as a joy and a blessing, not a right.' **(HildaW)**

Getting on with the other grandparents will make life easier. If you're friends, you are far more likely to bend over backwards to accommodate each other than to be fighting duels over the baked goods and the knitted blankets to oust each other from 'power'.

> 'Don't worry, love expands to embrace all the babies and all the grandparents – if you work to nurture it.' **(Ariadne)**

Rather than competing for the top slot, finding different roles to suit your strengths (and practicalities) can also be the key to family harmony. If you have the time, patience and inclination to look after small children while their parents work – then great. If you don't, find another way to get involved, be it babysitting in the evening, teaching the children skills like cooking, helping out with DIY, taking the little ones for walks at weekends ... the list is endless, and there are very few parents of young children who won't be grateful for an hour or two of respite.

It's true that sometimes being the paternal gran will mean a slower start. It's understandable that overwhelmed new mums can find the whole business of having a tiny baby a bit intimate and bewildering and prefer to share it with their own mum. But hang on in there. Don't fret that you're not getting as much time with the baby as the 'other' grandparents. Children go through phases and your time will come. That may be when they go through their brick-building phase, or their make-believe phase, or their Monopoly phase. If you stay interested and available, you will find a way to bond and become the special person who shares something they care about and that they will remember for the rest of their lives.

> 'We love spending time with them and are willing to help when we can. A granny who says, "What can I do to help?" will be very welcome.' **(wisewoman)**

GRANIMOSITY

> 'What is the difference between in-laws and outlaws? Outlaws are wanted! Just a joke – honest ...' **(grandmaagain)**

Relationships with the children and grandchildren might be everything you could wish for, but sometimes (and only sometimes) negotiating the relationships you have with the new in-laws (aka the 'other' grandparents, be they maternal or paternal) is a bit like climbing up K2. The hard way.

Welcome to the world of granimosity.

It's worth remembering that your grandchildren can have a great relationship with you *regardless* of the relationships they have with anyone else. There isn't only so much fun or love to go round. You are loved for who you are, not who someone else is. And it's not a competition!

> 'In the end, we have had our families, and now as grandparents we are there to enjoy the grandchildren – not compete with or envy the other grandparents. By and by, the grandchildren learn to appreciate you for who you are, and just want to enjoy you, however much or how little you see them.' (MDougall)

SPECIAL OCCASIONS

There's nothing nicer than special days or events, particularly if they involve a multigenerational get-together. But when it comes to taking turns, Christmas, Mother's Day and high days and holidays can feel more like the Battle of Agincourt than a series of loving celebrations. Once more unto the breach ...

CHRISTMAS

Your children have met someone and they're all loved up and then there's a baby and you're thrilled and everything ought to be great ... except they now have two families to please.

Yes, practicalities (distance, illness, etc.) might intervene with logistics, but for many (if not most) couples, which family to see and when is a headache that can begin months before.

Taking turns is obviously the fairest and simplest route. Alternating lets everyone know where they are, although it doesn't necessarily make your 'year off' any easier.

> 'I am trying VERY hard to be sensible and pragmatic about it – and Boxing Day works out a lot cheaper if there are a lot of us (and is so much easier), and at least we would see them all on the 26th. What's in a date after all? Can you tell that I am trying VERY hard?' (gracesmum)

One option, of course, is for both sets of grandparents to pitch up to share the day with the children and grandchildren, but if there's any sizeable travel distance, this either involves the expense of hotels or a home big enough to fit everyone in. And if both sets of grandparents have other children and grandchildren, this can quickly turn into something like a page out of *Where's Wally?*, with far too many people in far too confined a space.

If you can't all spend Christmas Day together, think about Boxing Day or New Year instead and perhaps do something different (*immediately starts making extravagant plans*) to take your mind off who's not with you on the day itself.

> 'Occasionally we are on our own for Christmas Day, and then we help at a lunch for the elderly and people alone, and that keeps everything firmly in perspective.'
> **(Ariadne)**

If you do find yourselves at home minus children and grandchildren on Christmas Day, you can always make it special with 'grown-up' food and drink (bring on the mai tais). Have some treats that may be too expensive or unsuitable for a larger family group or go to a restaurant and let someone else do the cooking (and better still, the washing-up). Enjoy not being bounced on by overexcited children at 4am. Relish having the remote control to yourselves. Plan a second Christmas where you can all get together and do the whole thing all over again. Any excuse to have another slap-up turkey dinner works for us.

> 'When all is said and done, it is only one day in the year and we have our families the other 364 days so it isn't worth getting upset about if they have other plans.' (grumpyoldwoman)

MOTHER'S DAY

Mother's Day is no less tricky, even though for most of us it has now become something other than the traditional Mothering Sunday. Yes, it's a day for mums to be fussed over and have treats (always something we quite like), but once you're a gran there are daughters and daughters-in-law who are now mums themselves to fit into the equation as well.

Does a mum or a wife take priority in the pampering stakes on Mother's Day? Of course customs vary from family to family, but the Gransnet consensus seems to be that, where there are small children, Daddy should be there to help them spoil their mum.

> 'I think it should be about the father teaching kids to show appreciation of their mothers.' (JessM)

This is not to say that there aren't some who also set great store by respecting their elders and making sure their mum (or mother-in-law) doesn't feel completely left out. Naturally, it may not be possible to get every generation of the family together, and in that case it's wise to be delighted that they remembered to send a card.

And you can always decide to side with the many who are highly sceptical of the whole thing anyway:

> 'I think it's just an artificially created day which makes a lot of money. It's how our sons treat us the rest of the year that matters.' (crimson)

WHEN THE FAMILY COME TO STAY

If your family live some distance away then, there are few things that can beat having them all to stay and being able to enjoy quality time with the grandchildren 24/7.

But families have a tendency to expand at precisely the time that many grandparents decide to downsize. So if you don't have guest rooms galore to accommodate your visitors, how best to make sure that everybody's happy and comfortable?

If you don't have enough space, don't feel bad. If the family has to sleep elsewhere, there's nothing to stop you hosting meals and welcoming them to your home during the day. Perhaps you have room for the grandchildren? So if it's not too much, why not let them stay while Mum and Dad book into a guesthouse or hotel nearby?

It's much easier to accommodate small children than grown-ups. (Though whether the children stay put during the night is another matter altogether ...)

> 'We moved from a bigger house to a much, much smaller house so when grandson aged five comes to stay now and then we really struggle. We have tried him on a single lilo at the side of our bed on the floor ... but he fidgets so much, he bangs his arms and legs on the wall, etc. ... so we have recently got a double lilo, which I put on the lounge floor then two sleeping bags on top, which he is always nice and cosy with. But this means poor Hubby is sent off to bed early and Grandma somehow ends up sleeping on 6 inches and clinging on for dear life on the edge of the lilo. Of course prior to bedtime this is a pirate's raft ready for the high seas (and, believe me, I feel like I have had a night on the high seas by the time morning comes!).'
> (bikergran)

Practical options that don't take up too much space are trundles that fit under beds, blow-up mattresses (make sure you get one with a motorised pump if you don't want to spend the bulk of the visit red-faced and wheezing), sofa cushions with sleeping bags, Z-beds and bedding rolls. If you don't have room to store them, ask around to see what you can borrow, or perhaps your visitors can bring their own. All of these options work well for children* and youngish adults, although they may not be ideal for older family members or those with bad backs. We speak from experience.

> 'When the work on our house is finished I will have two spare bedrooms and the study and second sitting room will double as makeshift bedrooms. But that is not an invitation for my children to breed like rabbits.'
> **(harrigran)**

If you do have room for everyone, then it's always wise to talk through the sleeping arrangements with your children to make sure they're as practical as possible. For example: having small children who might need the loo near the loo, putting small children with kamikaze tendencies as far away from stairs as possible and so on.

Should you give up your own bed to accommodate your visitors? If you're happy to do so and if you have a decent alternative, then it's fair enough. But, if you're being put under pressure when you're not very keen to do so, stand your ground. You may need to be functioning in the morning.

---

* With babies and very young children, it's essential to keep to safety recommendations.

HOW AND WHEN TO HELP YOUR ADULT CHILDREN

At what stage should your grown-up children be left to stand on their own two feet? How much emotional and practical support should you offer? Should you bail them out financially? (See page 44.) Should you be worrying about your children even when they have become parents themselves?

> 'When they ring and tell me about their problems, illnesses, pregnancies, mothers-in-law, baby troubles or whatever, I sympathise and offer advice and help and in some cases worry, but not half as much as I used to. We mums will never not care, but we have to learn to let go and let them get on with their own lives unencumbered by us ...' **(gally)**

Your children are among the people you love most in the world and it's natural to want them to be happy, healthy and settled. But it's easy to get too involved; sometimes it helps to stand back and remember they are now grown-ups who are able to take responsibility for themselves.

Apart from anything else, if they know you are worrying about them constantly, it becomes a stress and a burden for them too, which is somewhat counterproductive if all you wish for them is hassle-free happiness.

'My technique for distancing myself sufficiently from my children's problems is to think back to when I was their age and how I would have felt if I had thought my mother was constantly worrying about me, finding solutions to my problems or contacting me to check on my well-being. The answer is that I would have been exasperated and irritated that I was still being seen as a child who could not cope with and resolve the problems I have in life. It enables me to take a deep breath and step back.' **(FlicketyB)**

You can also find ways to keep yourself and your mind busy so there's no time to spend fretting. Anything that requires concentration works a treat – sudoku, crosswords, jigsaws – anything that lets you lose yourself in the moment. If you find yourself worrying about things that you know are really not that worrisome, it may be worth talking to your GP or seeing a counsellor to help you cope.

Sometimes, sadly, there are very real things to worry about – illness, broken relationships, redundancies, financial troubles, etc. – and then you have to judge how far to get involved, if at all.

'I live in a close family and will celebrate their successes and grieve with them, or worry when things are dire. When I left home to get married, I received very little support and found that daunting. There is a balance to be struck between cosseting and enabling our children to stand on their own two feet, but sometimes life's blows call for a family to rally round and help each other through.' (carol)

LIVING TOGETHER RATHER THAN MARRIAGE

Gone are the days when the 'right' thing to do was grow up, get married and have a baby, and living 'over the brush' was something no well-brought-up girl would ever consider.

Now, with the number of cohabiting couples with children the same as the number of married couples with children in the UK, there's a strong chance that at least one of your offspring will have a baby without having a ring on their finger.

If you're a traditionalist you may have doubts, but in terms of general acceptance, your grandchildren will fare no worse as part of a loving unmarried family than they would as part of one that's married.

Obviously, marriage matters to different people for different reasons. While worrying about what people might think should really no longer be a concern in the 21st century, for those with strong religious beliefs having a baby out of wedlock can be a more difficult thing to accept.

On a practical level, marriage does ensure certain rights including, inheritance, guardianship of children, etc., so it's important to have provisions in place for those who don't want to take the plunge but do want to start a family.

> 'I reckon a formal wedding is just a station on the train journey of a relationship. If you are both aiming towards the same destination, you will enjoy travelling in one another's company whether you have stepped out briefly at that stop and taken vows to stay together, or whether you travelled on regardless. The problems come when one or other party wants to change their ticket while there is still outstanding business – particularly when children are involved.' **(elegran)**

If the parents of your grandchild have decided not to marry, it's important that the baby's father is there to register his name on the birth certificate (which will ensure equal parental responsibility) and that both parents have made wills leaving their share of any property and assets to one another (which would happen automatically if they were married).

> 'Neither of my daughters are married to their long-term partners, even though they have children, and my husband and I do not have any problem with this, but I dread to think what our parents would have made of it! However, our sons-out-laws' parents do worry more than we do about it – afraid that if there was a split

> they might not be as involved with the grandchildren and their sons would lose their homes, as both our daughters are the bigger earners and sole not joint owners of their houses.' (Granny23)

Sadly the things we really don't want to think about often become the things we really wish we had thought about. Considering every eventuality isn't always pleasant, but it's usually wise, even if you're all destined to live happily ever after.

CHAPTER FOUR
CHILDCARE

'I am a nana (i.e. a grandma) not a nanny (i.e. a childcare professional).' (milliesmum)

More parents than ever are having to leave their children to go and earn a wage. And more parents than ever are finding it difficult – or impossible – to afford the soaring costs of childcare.

Small wonder then that a third of UK grandparents have ended up doing increased childcare since the recession began. Now around 5.8 million grandparents regularly look after little ones for an average of 10 hours a week. One recent estimate suggests that this is saving parents en masse over £11 billion a year. A third of all working families rely on grandparents to help out with the childcare, and a whopping 97 per cent of grandparents who get involved with the childcare don't get paid a penny.

ISSUES TO CONSIDER

So what if you're asked to do the Mary Poppins bit? You may, of course, jump at the chance of spending time with the grandchildren. You may even now be jogging round the block to get in training. You may be happy to do it because it's helpful to your own children, in which case we applaud you, in a slightly awed way. Or you may end up feeling you've been backed into a corner where you can't say no.

Helping out, even if you're happy to do it, can often turn out to be quite demanding (understatement alert), so make sure you're honest with yourself from the start about what may be expected of you and the effect this may have on your life. For example: are you in good health? Are your energy levels up to dealing with little ones? (That's approximately the energy of a subatomic particle in the Large Hadron Collider.) Do you have other commitments to work round, such as elderly parents, other children, volunteering? Do you work?

If you have a job and are being asked to look after grandchildren on top, make sure you've fully considered whether you're really happy to give up your free time. You will also need to think about how it may impact on your career or earning potential.

'Many years ago I took a part-time job in a school in order to have the holidays off with my own children.

I am now staying in the job because it fits in with my daughter's working life. Am I being unreasonable by telling them that now (after divorcing) I want to look for a full-time job (I'm only 53) and won't be able to look after their children during the week any more? How much free childminding is too much?' **(Ruislipnan)**

The answer to this is, of course, how long is a piece of string?

If you are happy to do it and you can afford to do it, great. If you have other demands on your time, or need to go out to work yourself, then there may come a point where you will just have to say no. Saving your children money but putting yourself into financial hardship to do so is never going to make sense.

It's hard for a family to afford a mortgage on one salary these days – assuming they can even get on the housing ladder. But does this mean that Granny should be left to pick up the pieces?

'When we were young mums, we didn't automatically expect our mothers to help on a regular basis with childcare ... did we? Yes, they helped us out if necessary, but it wasn't the norm. I looked after my own kids, as did all of my friends. The women at the school gates were the children's mothers not their grandmothers! The current generation of mothers want it all – kids, careers, beautiful homes, all the latest equipment, etc.,

> but it seems to me that it's their own mothers who are enabling them to have this lifestyle by giving up THEIR well-deserved freedom.' **(specki4eyes)**

A generation on, women work not only because they want to, but because they have to. The economic climate, exorbitant house prices and the ever-rising cost of living mean that, for many families, surviving on one wage – as might have been the norm not so very long ago – is no longer a realistic prospect.

Many find themselves having to work all hours simply to keep their heads above water, without luxuries and fancy holidays ever entering the equation. For some, decent childcare is something they simply can't afford, while, for others, leaving young children with trusted and much-loved family members makes it easier to bear than leaving them elsewhere.

But not everyone automatically wants the responsibility and commitment of caring for their grandchildren, however much they love them. If this is how you feel, then panic not – it's *not* just you.

> 'I have made it quite plain, I won't be providing free childcare, I have done all that three times already. Your children, you look after them. I have friends who do, and they are exhausted, fed up and feel put upon and feel they have to run their lives around their grandchildren ... No thanks!' **(Fallon8)**

SET OUT THE PARAMETERS

If you are one of the nearly 6 million who are happy (or at least willing) to help on a regular basis, make sure you have thought through (and set out) the parameters *before* you start. For example, what happens if you want to take a holiday? The last thing you want to find when your own children are all grown up is that you are back to being tied to the (hideously expensive) school holidays to take a break.

If you are helping out one child with their kids, will there be repercussions from other children who will expect similar time spent on them?

If you're part of the ever-growing 'stretched middle' and have elderly parents to care for as well as grand-children, what might you need to do for them that could compromise a regular childcare commitment?

The other thing to bear in mind is that people get sick, at any age. Grandparents looking after small children – aka germ magnets – are more than likely to pick up bugs galore. When this happens – and it will – what contingencies have your children put in place? It's the parents' responsibility, not yours, to sort this out, and it certainly won't do you or anyone else any good to have to get off your sickbed to spend a day toddler-taming or standing in a rainy playground. Apart from anything else, it's not a bad thing for people (i.e. family) to have to take a step back and realise that you're only human.

'Last Christmas Day I fell on the ice at my daughter's house and broke my wrist. Because I have been out of action, at last people are NOT assuming I will help! If my eldest grandson's dog gets hurt, someone else is roped in for transport. And if someone needs the A&E, there's a bus!' (Oxon70)

LOOKING AFTER GRANDCHILDREN CAN BE EXHAUSTING

A survey conducted in 2012 showed that a toddler's daily antics burn the equivalent energy to an adult running an entire marathon. Or cycling 82 miles. Or doing 83 rounds in a boxing ring. Or climbing a mountain *twice* the height of Ben Nevis (which stands at 1,344m if you'd like the stats to hand to prove your point). Frankly, we need a lie-down at the very thought, but the bottom line is that looking after small children can be very, *very* tiring indeed.

However much you may adore them, it's a job and a half. It's exhausting when you are a parent. And it's even more exhausting when you're another twenty or thirty years down the line.

'I'm always tired after having my two little granddaughters for the day. My daughter says I'm permanently 47 in her mind – I wonder how many of us have kids who think the same way and have genuinely (or conveniently) forgotten how old their parents really are!' (Hillary)

It's been pointed out more than once on our forums that the menopause is nature's way of telling us that the time has passed for bearing and bringing up babies and small children. And to make matters worse it's not only the physical running around, clearing up and bottom wiping that takes its toll. The responsibility of caring for any child who is not your own (related or not) can be stressful, particularly with little ones who have a habit of getting up to all sorts the very second your back is turned.

'When looking after your own children you just do the best you can. When it's your children's children ... it somehow is so much more important to do everything right. There is this ever-present worry of what if something goes wrong?' (HildaW)

However much you love being with your grandchildren, if it wears you out, then say so. Make sure that you build 'recovery' time into your week if you need it and that this can be accommodated in any plans you agree to.

If you do find yourself sighing with relief when they've gone, don't feel guilty. They may well be the most precious and adorable children in the known universe, but that doesn't stop them having the capacity to be utterly exhausting.

> 'My husband always jokes that he's seen the wonderful lights of Las Vegas and the bright lights of Blackpool, but the lights that bring the most joy are the back lights of our son's car going down the drive taking our grandchildren home.' **(saga)**

THINGS TO DO WITH GRANDCHILDREN

Long days with small children can be very long indeed if it's just you, them and a couple of stuffed toys for company. If looking after the grandchildren is a regular thing, it's best to make plans to add some form of structure to your day. The activities don't have to cost much (if anything) and they don't have to involve going far. Even the most adorable small child can have days of being ~~horrendous~~ *less than adorable* and sometimes a bit of company can mean the difference between saving your sanity and leaving it in tatters.

Because that's the thing – spending time with your grandchild en famille is very different to spending time with them when the rest of the grown-ups aren't around. Looking after little people can be lonely if you don't have anyone to hang out with, and it's a lot more tiring when there's no one else to hand them over to when you have had enough.

Activities, obviously, will depend on the age of the child. For very little ones there is likely to be a decent variety of classes and groups on offer. Don't be put off by any labelled 'Mother and baby/toddler' – they are just as likely to be filled with a selection of other carers, including grandparents.

> 'If my experience is anything to go by you will find lots of grandparents at toddler groups and playgroups. They are usually the "hands-on" ones who get down and play with the children!' **(wisewoman)**

Other activities worth looking into are messy play, soft play, music and dance classes. If you have a local Sure Start Centre, that's a great place to start, otherwise try library noticeboards, local newspapers and Gransnet Local for listings of what's available in your area.

Many libraries run free song sessions for under-twos and other activities for bigger children. Community centres, church halls and similar venues are also good places to find stay-and-play sessions or classes.

When you're back home don't worry about organising every minute of the time you spend together. Going with the flow or finding things that keep them happy while you can have a bit of a breather can work every bit as well as a day planned out with military precision.

> 'It's all very simple: toys, books, hugs and kisses. I found a little Barney thrown in very helpful as it can be quite fun and helps with the old A.B.C. and life skills (though I am sure there will be objections from some about looking at the telly).' **(POGS)**

In our book a bit of TV never did anyone any harm. Moderation in all things, as they say. There's no shame in needing the occasional pit stop to regroup and grab a cuppa. Indeed, if you're having them for longer than a couple of hours, then pacing yourself can be key.

DAMAGE LIMITATION

Small children (even babies) and mess go together like Morecambe and Wise, apple pie and custard, cheese and biscuits, tea and cake (ah, now you're talking ...).

House proud? If the answer is yes, then you may want to consider looking after the children on their own turf rather than yours. Your hopes of getting anything done at home will likely be dashed by constant demands for attention, bottom wiping, food, etc. in any case. This way you won't spend the next week getting everything back in order just in time for them to come and wreck the joint again.

> 'I have to reset my central heating, turn the phone back off mute, retrieve the remote control from the dog's basket, reset my cooker and washing machine, find my electric toothbrush and hope it's in the washing basket not down the toilet, take numerous plastic toys off the dog because she's found them in her bowl of water, put my knitting back on the needles, remove cookie dough from the back door where it was flung when we made

cookies and wipe up the water that was thrown all over the kitchen floor when four little hands "helped" me wash the dishes ... Another happy afternoon with my twin three-year-old grandsons.' **(carol)**

OVERNIGHT CHILDCARE

'Our children just assume that since we routinely cared for them and their siblings for years on end it should be a doddle for us to step in now to see to their offspring. But we know better, don't we?" **(learnergran)**

Day care is one thing; the overnight care of babies and toddlers is an entirely different kettle of fish. If you cherish your eight hours a night, the thought of being up and down with teething babies, fractious toddlers and small children who wake at the crack of dawn claiming it's morning and time to play may send you running for the hills.

Getting up in the night is tough enough when you're young. And it certainly doesn't get any easier two (or three, or four) decades later.

'Sometimes our children just don't think. They expect us to be just as active, capable and inexhaustible as we were when they themselves were young, and they won't accept that as we get older we just can't take on the challenges that we once did without a second thought.' **(yogagran)**

Having one small child to stay might be fine, but for many grandparents more than one at a time can be a bridge too far. Saying no to a request might not be what the parents want to hear, but it's the responsible thing to do if you feel it's going to be too much to cope with.

If you do have the stamina – or at least time to sleep it off the day after – then doing the night shift for parents with a newborn can offer the most precious gift there is (sleep!) and spending the wee small hours with a tiny grandchild can be a special bonding time for you both.

> 'My daughter and son-in-law are amazed and so grateful that I offer to give them a night off. But, oh, that precious, quiet time with my smiley little granddaughter showing her the stars and moonlight ... And the pleasure of getting back into bed knowing (hoping) she will sleep soundly for the next three hours, or four if I'm really lucky!' (GrandmaRoo)

WHEN TO SAY NO

If you have planned to spend your retirement playing bridge, learning to hang-glide, backpacking to Burma or even lying in bed all day reading books and eating violet creams, being a childminder – paid or unpaid – is likely to lead to some resentment, however much you love your children and grandchildren.

If spending time with them is what you'd choose to do in any case, then taking over some of the childcare arrangements can almost be a bonus, but being realistic about what you really want to do (not to mention what you actually *can* do) is vital.

There may be times when you feel unappreciated or taken advantage of, in which case a gentle word is the best place to start. But if you realise that the arrangement isn't working for you, then say so before any further damage is done.

> 'I provide wrap-around care for two of my grandchildren and neither expect nor receive any recompense. At times I would love to be off and doing my own thing, but there is an understanding that when my daughter is not here, I am, and I would much rather that than see them go off to a childminder at the crack of dawn and then after-school clubs not getting home until it was bedtime. I think we as grandmothers just need our daughters to be a little more considerate at times, but I suppose that's life and we all get complacent with those close to us.' (glassortwo)

Some grandparents find being on emergency call is more than enough.

> 'While I would lie down in front of a bus for my grandchildren if I thought it necessary, I also value my space/time/sanity.' (gracesmum)

But there is no norm and the golden rule is do only what you feel comfortable with and don't be pressured into any more than you know you can cope with. This will work out best for everyone in the long run.

> 'My daughter and son-in-law asked if we would care for our grandson on two days a week (7am to 7pm) and he would then go to nursery for one day a week. After a lot of thought we agreed to only have him for one day a week, so he was sent to nursery for the other two days. None of us has ever regretted this decision – he has benefited greatly from being at an excellent nursery, and we enjoy so much looking after him on Tuesdays. This way his parents don't feel they are taking advantage of us and we don't feel that we are being "put upon". I'm not at all sure we could manage two days – one is enough, it takes two to get over it! Honesty at the outset worked for us.' (riclorian)

This goes for babysitting and not just daytime childcare.

> 'I'm happy to help out when I can ... but I blinked and suddenly found myself stuck in every Saturday night with a toddler while his parents painted the town red. That's when I went on strike.' (marina)

If you're happy to spend your evenings in front of the telly, then doing so on their sofa instead of your own isn't the end of the world (especially if they have decent biscuits in). But if it means having to stay up late when you'd rather be in bed, or your children having a social life at the expense of your own, it's time to put your foot down.

> 'Being a grandmother isn't just about babysitting – it's about having a relationship with another generation, sharing fun times and passing on some wisdom ...'
> (mollie)

SHOULD YOU CHARGE FOR LOOKING AFTER YOUR GRANDCHILDREN?

If our forums are anything to go by, this is a controversial and thorny issue. There are many factors that come into play, including whether you're looking at a temporary or a permanent arrangement, whether you are happy to be helping out or if it's a necessity, whether the parents can afford to pay and, perhaps most importantly, whether looking after your grandchildren will affect you financially.

> 'Get real and stop fretting about a few bob, give your time unconditionally. When you are old and dribbling will you pay your daughter to wipe your face?'
> (nannajeannie)

A fair point perhaps, but, of course, it's not that simple.

If you need to earn money and are having to turn down paid work to do childcare, then, yes, you should be compensated. Ending up out of pocket should never be part of the package.

> 'My daughter's mother-in-law has two jobs – school dinners and after-school club several times a week. She is a widow and would suffer financially by reducing her hours, so my daughter and son-in-law will pay her the same wage to take care of our little granddaughters. They all get the best deal, and my granddaughters will be in good hands. I'll do my bit with weekends, babysitting in the evening or helping the mother-in-law out when she needs an extra pair of hands. Happy babies and happy parents.' **(whenim64)**

Just bear in mind that if your arrangement is formalised by payment for the childcare it will, of course, change things. Even if the income might be the decider between agreeing to do the childcare or not, it's likely to mean less flexibility for you than if it's a goodwill arrangement.

> 'I loved being with the grandchildren and felt lucky to be able to do so but also felt tired and subconsciously wished I could be doing something else, occasionally. Sometimes the responsibility for them seems endless at a time when there are other things I would like to be

doing. Perhaps the money isn't the real issue? More a case of being taken for granted?' **(crimson)**

Are they paying you because you are their first choice for childcare or because you are a cheap (or easy) option? Again, this will have repercussions. If you are enabling them to work and they wouldn't otherwise be able to do so, they will need to make sure that the terms suit you every bit as much as they suit them.

Even if they are topping up your pension to do something you would happily do anyway, remember that money changing hands can make things awkward when there's emotional investment too.

By paying you, your children effectively become your employers as well as your own flesh and blood. You have rights, they will naturally have expectations. They will want to think they are getting a good deal. You won't want to feel you are being ripped off. So make sure you're all on the same page and you've agreed terms in advance.

Costs such as food, outings and classes/groups should always be considered too. Other than treats and gifts, there is no reason not to expect expenses to be met by the parents, and if they've asked you to take them to an activity or on a day out then you should never feel forced to foot the bill.

'I think to reimburse the grandparents' expenses is an appropriate gesture – I also think that if they don't need the money they are right to turn it down. What to do? Give them a treat every now and again as a gesture of thanks and goodwill.' (grannyactivist)

THE GOING RATE

With childminders charging an average of £30+ a day, nurseries £11,000 a year and nannies around £10 an hour, childcare has become big business. It's small wonder that many families struggle to pay for what they need.

But there's no such thing as a going rate for grandparents and so if you are getting paid to look after the children, it's a matter of agreeing on what works for them and for you.

'I look after my youngest grandchild five days a week, while our son and his wife are at work, hours dependent upon what shift my son is on that week. I love doing it, but I do get paid, £1 an hour, which still saves them an awful lot of money in childcare fees, and also gives me a teeny bit of financial independence. I divide the money between my purse (for shopping), the holiday savings and my personal "spence".' (numberplease)

Some parents prefer to pay simply to keep the arrangement formal – as it would be with a childminder – in order that everyone knows where they are.

'My daughter insists on paying me when I look after her two little ones, both when she is working and when she and her husband are having an evening out. She insists because she says it then means that she can ask me any time and I am nearly always available. She also says she would far rather I look after them than someone else whom they don't know. I do have guilt about accepting it but am on a very low income and I also really appreciate the little extra.' (Ameliaanne)

Whatever you decide upon between you, don't forget to agree the ground rules up front and think ahead to scenarios where things might change (such as them earning more, you needing more downtime and so on). If you are looking after the children because you need the income, it's perfectly reasonable to expect the odd pay rise when the parents get one too.

If you don't need the money, then, whether you feel you should be compensated for your help or not, you may have to ask yourself whether it's worth upsetting the apple cart for the sake of a few pounds you can easily live without.

'I was happy to help my daughter get back on her feet with a job by offering to drop off/collect the grandchildren from school and looking after them till she got home. But now she has moved on to a job with better pay, so I think she should pay me more to look after them. She'd have to pay a childminder at least £400 a month for wrap-around care and, as she can afford this, I think she should pay the same to me. I raised this recently and my daughter felt it was unfair as she says she is still re-establishing her life and "expected" help from us as we had offered it. To be honest we don't need extra money and it's not as though I'd prefer to be doing anything else as the grandchildren are my life, but I wonder if I'm being taken for a ride?' **(granbo)**

The consensus, we've found, is that a little appreciation for your help goes a long way and that feeling put upon and unappreciated is not good for any relationship. But if you don't need the money and it's not compensation for wages that would otherwise be earned, making financial demands can be a cause for many resentful rows.

'It's okay to say no to childcare if the time/cost/ responsibility are too much. For whatever reason. It's okay to have additional costs for meals/petrol/outings reimbursed. I agree with the concept of regularly reviewing childcare arrangements to ensure they're still appropriate/convenient/achievable. But I can't get anywhere near understanding why any grandparent would seek recognition of the time they are devoting to their grandchildren.' **(notsogrand)**

It would be fair to say that the nation runs on a hidden army of grandparents who cover not only regular childcare, but also emergencies such as sick children, unavoidable appointments and occasions like public-sector strikes where schools and nurseries close.

> 'But our contribution to keeping the economy moving yet again goes unrecognised perhaps because we have no clout – I am sure there would be a very poor response to a strike call for grandparents.' **(Granny23)**

Of course in an ideal world childcare vouchers could be used for grandparents and not just registered minders and nurseries, and expenses incurred (such as petrol – many grandparents travel great distances to help out) would be tax deductible. But, naturally, nothing is ever quite that simple.

In any case, grans often take the view that accepting payment would distort the relationship.

> 'I would hate to be paid for looking after my grandchildren. It would change the way I feel. This is something I do out of love. It is a gift and I can't imagine it being put on a financial footing.' **(sneetch)**

In the meantime, if you're reluctant to take money from well-paid children but are giving up your free time (and energy) to look after the little ones, this is one suggestion we really liked:

> 'Why not suggest they could pay for your cleaning/gardening/dog walking to be done while you look after their children? That way you will not be exhausted and they get the best childcare in the world.' (Babyjack)

*

In short: do only what you can do, are happy to do and are confident in doing, be it caring for one or more grandchildren, day or night. Make sure you are all starting out with the same expectations and that you review arrangements regularly and if circumstances change. Remember small resentments can grow to become very large resentments if nothing is done. Most of all, enjoy the time you get to spend with your grandchildren, they have a nasty habit of growing up way too fast.

> 'Looking after them I can get very tired and sometimes feel a bit put on (my own worst enemy), but I have had the opportunity to be such a big part of their childhood and really I love it ... but don't tell my daughter.' (glassortwo)

CHAPTER FIVE
SMALLER GRANDCHILDREN

'My lovely granddaughter asked me, "Nanny, why do walk with a stick? Is it because your boobies are so big you would fall over if you didn't have it?" I could see the look on my son-in-law's face – very guilty.' (POGS)

DEALING WITH FUSSY EATERS

Some children will happily eat anything that's put in front of them. Others will refuse to countenance anything other than fish fingers and dolly mixtures till they reach their teens. There's an element of luck involved. (Hands up if there are foods *you* hate with a passion? Yes, us too. And some of us just have more than others.) But it's a rare parent or grandparent who doesn't worry when a small but very firm child refuses point-blank to eat anything that's vaguely good for them.

Getting children to actually try things is often half the battle. There will be plenty of times when you are rewarded with a 'Bleurgggh, that's yuck' (usually accompanied by dramatic retching noises), but there will be others when they just might surprise themselves by liking something they have previously declared inedible.

Of course tastes do change over time, but the earlier you can get a child into the habit of healthy-ish eating, the easier it will be for all of you. Sometimes being that step removed can actually work in your favour. It's quite often the case that children will try stuff for Granny that they'd never try for their parents. So there's at least a chance you might have success where everyone else has failed.

You also have the benefit of hindsight. It's likely your own children went through similar phases (something they will likely have forgotten or strenuously deny), and if they came through them okay in the end it's much easier to see the wood for the trees in this situation too. Ah, the wisdom of grans.

Decent nutrients are, of course, essential for any growing child, so if they're continuing to refuse point-blank to put anything suspiciously healthy near their mouths, then resorting to disguising food may be your answer (until they realise that they do actually like it after all).

> 'It's remarkable what you can "hide" in a basic Bolognese or even a tomato sauce. We have got away with carrots, spinach, courgettes, broccoli and plenty more. You'll find that your hand blender is your friend ...' (Minnieapolis)

It can be extremely stressful when a toddler will happily eat biscuits and snacks until the cows come home, yet proper mealtimes turn into a battleground. If this is the case, it's not always easy to find things that will tempt them and at the same time reassure you that they're getting all the goodness they need.

It's a faff, yes, but arranging food to look attractive on the plate can work wonders. Sausages leaning against a mound of mashed potato make an entirely convincing castle guarded by soldiers. And the whole olives for eyes, grated carrots for hair thing can be fun.

Letting children – even very little ones – help with preparation can also give them an incentive to eat something healthy:

> 'My granddaughter and I used to make green soup by, basically, blending up frozen peas (cook them first in microwave!)' (JessM)

We can also highly recommend orange soup (butternut squash), red soup (tomato) and indeed traffic-light soup – a combination of pea, butternut squash and tomato soups in one bowl.

> 'Miniature veg and fruit often appeals to small children too – baby sweetcorn, cherry tomatoes, satsumas, tiny seedless grapes, blueberries, etc. Similarly, mini pizza, for example, can have tomato and other veg as part of the topping. Let your grandchild choose the toppings from a judicious selection. If she's "made" it herself, she'll probably eat it. Whatever you do, don't make a fuss about eating fruit and veg or any other food type, for that matter, as you will be making a rod for your own back.' **(absentgrana)**

There's nothing wrong with insisting that a reluctant child has at least *a taste* of something they don't like and that they have proclaimed they are never going to eat, ever. You can whisk it away after the merest tip-of-the-tongue effort. What seems slimy and lumpy (rice pudding) at two may be delicious (sweet, creamy) at ten.

SNACKS

On the snack front, going cold turkey (as it were) may prove impossible, but cutting down on snacks will mean little ones are more likely to eat the things you want them to at mealtimes in the end. Don't push things they really don't like. But if they're hungry and they realise there's nothing else, it's far more likely that you'll get a result.

'Don't offer alternatives if they turn their nose up at what is on offer. Just shrug and take it away. Toddlers try hard to manipulate and manage their parents (and grandparents!), but they don't tend to starve themselves once they realise there are no sweet things and crisps on offer.' (JessM)

If snacks are the only way forward in the short term, make them healthy ones. Rice cakes, wholegrain cereal, chopped-up veg, blueberries and grapes (cut in half) are all perfect treats for toddlers, and, if they are filling up on these, at least you know they're also getting some goodness.

And remember that, generally:

'Faddiness doesn't last forever, although it feels like it at the time.' (carol)

EATING OUT

Eating out should be a pleasure, a treat for a special occasion or when you are too tired to cook, fancy trying something new or simply want a change of scene. However, with small children a lovely, relaxing meal in a restaurant can be anything but lovely and relaxing.

But, before you clamp yourself firmly to the kitchen table till the small fry hit double figures, may we assure you that there's no need to panic. Yes, it goes without saying that if a toddler decides to have an all-out meltdown and lie screaming on the floor, resisting all attempts to remove them, then your experience may be somewhat marred. And while this can – and does – happen to the best of us, we've found with the right preparation and organisation eating out with little ones really can be something that the whole family will enjoy.

WHERE TO EAT OUT

Choosing the right place is key. You know you are going to be fairly safe with most of the major chains whose business is primarily aimed at families, but with independent restaurants, hotels, cafes and the like it's always worth a quick advance call to check that it's going to be suitable. For example, do they have high chairs? Balancing an active baby with a fist full of chewed-up bread on your knee while you try to hold on to them, eat your own meal and move knives, salt and pepper and all manner of other lethal tableware out of the reach of small hands does not a relaxing experience make. We speak from (bitter) experience.

Does the restaurant have a children's menu? If they don't, are they happy to serve smaller portions of any suitable adult dishes? If not, it can work out expensive to pay full whack for a huge plate of food when the likelihood is that once it arrives: (a) the small child will decide they didn't want that in the first place; or (b) they will eat six peas and a piece of bread but dismiss everything else as 'yucky'; or (c) they will want what you've got and you're now lumbered with something you hate. On which note – ordering dishes to share can work well, not least because it removes the angst associated with options (a) and (c), plus by eating your half with great relish you might just be able to convince them that (b) is no longer on the agenda either.

If you are taking very small ones along, are there baby-changing facilities that you can use? This one is probably top of our list of essentials. We are still scarred (several years down the line) by an exploding-nappy-small-cubicle-no-sink-no-mat-no-nothing experience that involved a complex on-the-knee-with-a-clump-of-toilet-paper debacle, resulting in a slipped disc and two people leaving the establishment without trousers. One was small enough to get away with it, the other was thankful for a very long jumper but still needed several gins to recover.

Don't ever rely on a restaurant to provide amenities to keep small children occupied while you wait for your food. Even those that generally do sometimes won't. At one busy chain restaurant we were eventually, and rather grudgingly, given one crayon for three children to share because all the rest were 'in use'.

Small pads and packs of pens, pencils and crayons weigh very little and easily fit in a handbag and can truly make the difference between sanity and being too embarrassed ever to return to a favourite eaterie. Pound shops are often a great source of goodies for such occasions.

If you're eating out with a child with allergies, it's definitely worth a quick phone call (or online check) before you go. We've found a huge diversity in what major chains have to offer. Some have special allergy menus with plenty of alternatives suggested in order to avoid certain ingredients, others do little in order to accommodate.

Independent cafes and restaurants that don't offer special menus or dietary information online are often very helpful, although many places are unable to guarantee that there will be no cross-contamination.

Don't worry, it's absolutely doable. But this is definitely one situation where Baden-Powell was bang on the money. Always, always be prepared.

As for getting the kids to behave while you're out, often one of granny's 'looks' is enough to stop any mischief in its tracks.

> 'And in addition to my "stare" we used "ABC", which stood for Attitude, Behaviour, Change! Seemed to work, the child was warned/admonished without public humiliation!' **(phoenix)**

And, finally, some hygiene advice.

'I avoid anywhere that has salad bars set out because they have been shown to have traces of faeces and urine in them, unless you are the first in the queue when the plastic is taken off! Don't eat peanuts which are displayed on a bar, either!' **(greatnan)**

Still hungry? No, we thought not.

TRAVELLING AND FLYING WITH GRANDCHILDREN

Keeping small children occupied on long journeys is definitely something it pays to plan ahead. There's not much you can do when you realise that magazines, stickers and snacks would have been a good idea if you are already sealed in a metal tube 30,000 feet over the Bay of Biscay.

There's a wide range of things worth including in your hand luggage:

'My daughter has a travel DVD player and plays *Bob the Builder*, *Peppa Pig* and *Mr Tumble* over and over on long journeys.' **(carol)**

An iPad (switched to flight mode where appropriate) can also be great. It doesn't weigh too much or take up a lot of room and can be a great source of TV programmes (download programmes via the BBC iPlayer app for free and they'll 'last' for up to 30 days), games and other activities. There are also lots of free apps and downloads available to appeal to small children.

Stickers are brilliant for little ones and an endless source of fun. Just be prepared for strange looks at passport control. We've found that managing to remove everything they've stuck all over you is a hit-and-miss affair.

There's a great selection of children's magazines on the market and these can be a perfect treat for the journey. Some of the activities within them may need your help (depending on the ages of the children), but even browsing should keep them happily occupied for a while. There's usually stuff to colour in too so don't forget to keep a small pack of crayons, pens or pencils handy.

If you're travelling long haul, most airlines have seat-back TVs. If the child is under two years of age, bear in mind that they won't have their own seat, so could end up watching your telly instead. Even if they're older, be prepared for your own viewing to be interrupted by a fair amount of wriggling, headphone dropping and endless questions about whatever they're 'watching'.

Also:

'Make sure you have their favourite blanket and cuddly packed in a bag ... so you can produce it as soon as you are seated. I have recently done several long-haul

> flights with babies/toddlers on board ... they've all been very good ... so ask cabin staff for advice too!' (Jacey)

Avoid taking: any toys that make a noise (unless you want to be lynched by the other passengers); toys with lots of bits (we can guarantee you will lose at least one crucial part) anything fiddly or likely to roll off the table – as scrabbling under airline (or train) seats is (a) nigh on impossible, (b) not a good look and (c) recommended only if you want to spend your children's entire inheritance on osteopath fees.

> 'When one of my grandchildren was flying back from Australia with his parents I made up a bag full of little wrapped presents for him to open – one every hour or so when he got bored – things like a little car, a crayon and book, a little pack of plasticine, a finger puppet, etc. Once I had collected lots of wee things I wrapped them individually so he could have the fun of unwrapping. It worked very well.' (wisewoman)

Ideas like this are great for children who can't sit still or have short attention spans. You can also try games (according to the age of the child), although 'I Spy' does become somewhat repetitive in a confined space, such as an airline cabin. Once you've done S for seat, C for cloud and T for table, there's not a whole lot else to choose from. In a car or on a train, where you can see a changing landscape out of the window, you might fare rather better.

Do try to think outside the box. We once spent an inordinate amount of time on a railway platform trying to work out what, other than chair, could possibly begin with 'ch'. The answer, from a *very* smug four-year-old was: 'Easy – ch-rain ch-racks.' Still, it was at least a valuable lesson in improving our enunciation.

> 'You can also do the first one to spot a red car, pylon, whatever. Or someone start a story and next player continues it.' **(ninathenana)**

> 'I've always thought it's a bit much expecting very young children to cope with travelling in cars on their own and whenever it's been possible an adult has always sat in the back seat with them. It's usually me and for the grandchildren we've used things like "fuzzy felt" lift-the-flap books, appropriate story CDs (oh, the memory of travelling down to Devon one year playing *Fantastic Mr Fox* over and over).' **(HildaW)**

It's a very good idea to take food along with you too, rather than relying on what you can pick up on a train or plane. Sandwiches are great for small children who might not like the meals that are otherwise on offer. Small boxes of raisins and dried fruit work well too, as do breadsticks and plain biscuits, such as Rich Tea, etc.

Don't take things that are messy, likely to melt or are too rich or greasy and may induce nausea.

On which note, do take:

> 'A change of clothes. Better still two changes of clothes. For them AND for you. I am the voice of bitter experience.' (margareth)

A very good point. You never know if small children might be sick or spill something on themselves – or, worse, on you. Grown-ups 'wearing' airline blankets while disembarking is not a good look at all.

If you are off on a lengthy journey, it's a good idea to let smaller children work off as much energy as possible in the airport or station. Not only will this mean you have a better chance of them sitting still en route, but it might also wear them out so much that they'll sleep. This is definitely the key to a quiet and stress-free trip!

KEEPING THE LITTLE ONES AMUSED

Of course it's not just on journeys that small children need occupying. If you look after or visit little grandchildren on a regular basis, then it's a great idea to have an array of activities up your sleeve that don't cost the earth, or, better still, are free. You also need some activities that work on the rainiest of days. Things that will keep them happy but leave you (vaguely) sane.

Local listings are invaluable when it comes to finding out what's going on in your area. (Have you tried Gransnet Local yet?) Most places have activities and groups to appeal to a wide range of ages and interests and many don't cost a bean.

Are there museums or galleries within easy reach? These are often free and many lay on activities especially for children, particularly at weekends and during school holidays.

Parks are always a winner, especially if you take a picnic, although they're not ideal for wet weather. One top tip: if you're braving the local playground after the rain has stopped, take an old bath towel along with you. It can take ages for equipment to dry and swabbing it down yourself is highly recommended if you don't want to spend the rest of the day with a damp behind. Jumping in puddles on the way home is always fun for children (okay, and grandparents) of all ages. Don't forget everyone's wellies though.

On wet or winter days why not go and choose books to borrow from the local library? Or Play-Doh, a rolling pin and a load of cutters can keep little hands happily occupied for hours on end.

'Collect a drawer full of things like farm animals and drawing materials, old greeting cards that you can cut out

> shapes from and stick on to scrap paper to make pictures. Collect bits and bobs that fascinate children – my twin grandsons love mooching through a tin of odd scraps and odd objects and using them in imaginative play.' **(Carol)**

Everyday objects or bits and bobs you might find around the house can provide hours of fun. Littlies love old boxes or pots and pans they can bang with wooden spoons, etc. Bigger ones might enjoy making their own glue from flour and water or creating papier mâché using old newspapers. The contents of the recycling box can provide hours of fun with a bit of spin: forget 'rubbish' – it's all about 'junk modelling'.

> 'Potato prints. Masks made from paper plates. Rolls of discounted wallpaper liner – terrific for going "large" with pictures, prints, etc. ... and, if you can, try to plan out the day ahead of time (not always easy, I know) – with plenty of "quiet time" if you can manage it while you catch your breath.' **(butternut)**

Paints are usually a winner, but, top tip: make sure you go for washable ones. Red streaks are always better when they have been removed from favourite tops and the sofa, rather than when they're still in evidence many months later.

Always remember to make sure that toys and equipment are age-appropriate and safe. While bigger children may still enjoy the chance to play with younger children's things, toys intended for older children can present safety issues (such as choking hazards) for smaller siblings or cousins and should be kept well away from the little ones.

Small children often love 'helping' with cleaning, sweeping and dusting. (Strange how quickly they grow out of this. Embrace it while you can.) If all else fails, there's always baking. (See how we always manage to bring things back round to cake?)

We've touched on TV elsewhere (see page 108), but unless the parents have expressly said switching it on is on pain of death, don't feel bad about taking a breather while the wee ones have a bit of downtime in front of the screen. Gone are the days when *Watch with Mother* was your only option. Now there's a whole range of fantastic programmes available on most channels and for all ages that are educational and enjoyable too. (Sometimes a little bit too enjoyable ...)

> 'Confession ... Over the Christmas/New Year break my daughter and son-in-law were off work so they looked after the granddaughter. I was a bit bored one day and found myself doing a catch-up online 'cos I missed watching *Chuggington, Bob the Builder, Rastamouse* and *Charley Bear*!' **(PoppaRob)**

Oh, and if they're not your cup of tea it's probably best to keep that to yourself.

'Some of our viewing habits (and my thoughts on some shows) have definitely rubbed off on the granddaughter. My daughter reported that they were visiting friends and the friends' toddler mentioned Angelina Ballerina. Granddaughter piped up "Angelina Ballerina is a pretentious rat!"' (PoppaRob)

Other activities that have stood the test of time, and that will go down as well with grandchildren as they did with your own children, include waving at trains (always a bonus when the drivers wave back), a bus ride or:

'Looking at machinery, preferably moving machinery. Building sites are compulsive viewing and the activity only limited by how long you are willing to stand around peering at JCBs.' (JessM)

READING TO GRANDCHILDREN

Surely one of the greatest joys of grandparenting is curling up with a small child and a good book. Getting them into reading (or at least being read to) early is a great way to encourage a love of books for life, and discovering old favourites and new is fantastic however old you are.

Books help children to learn about new things and experiences, and to develop their vocabulary and imagination. Plus reading together is a lovely way to give a little one some undivided attention.

> 'Sit close enough to have a cuddle at the same time and also then you will both be able to see the book. A book without too much reading on each page – a couple of lines and also interesting pictures with details.' **(Bez)**

In fact do make the most of the pictures. Use them to discuss the story and what else might be happening around it. Point to objects they might not know and name them – it's a great way to pick up new words.

It's worth remembering that repetition can be as appealing to small children as it is unappealing to their parents and grandparents. Brace yourself for having to read the same book over and over again (and again and again). Rhymes are oddly easier for this – there's a reason why Dr Seuss and Julia Donaldson have such a powerful appeal to grown-ups as well as children. However tempting it might be, don't zip through the pages in a desperate effort to get them to move on to something else. Take it slowly.

It can be fun to involve the little ones in the story too. Try changing the name of the central character to your grandchild's name. There's nothing little ones like more than thinking the book is all about them.

> 'And my grandchildren love me to "do the voices", which I think helps make the book come to life for them. I really don't think there is a right way or wrong way to

read with them. Just try to enjoy it yourself and they will too.' (Gillybob)

DISCIPLINE

'They don't make parents like they used to, do they?' (nanafrancis)

The behaviour of small children – acceptable and unacceptable – is something that comes up almost daily on our forums and raises many, many questions.

IS IT OKAY TO GIVE IN FOR AN EASY LIFE?

Consensus – generally no. Breaking bad habits early will make for a much easier time later on.

'Let them see what is expected from them. If you let them win at age one, I dread to think what other battles you are going to have over their childhood.' (glassortwo)

This is a question often raised over the issue of small children migrating from their own beds into those of their parents (and grandparents). Unless you are happy to share (and a number of people are, though we can only assume their children/grandchildren are less wriggly than ours), it's always advisable to look at whether there is a reason behind the change in behaviour before making a major issue of it.

Marriage break-ups, bereavements, starting nursery or school, even general anxiety can all affect small children as much as big ones, and stress can often manifest itself in nocturnal visits. Bad dreams or feeling unwell can have small fry scurrying into bed with you. Equally they may turn up due to nothing more than a desire to hang out with MumDad/Granny in the wee small hours.

Whatever the reason, it's best not to make a big issue of it. Tend or comfort if that's what's needed. Otherwise pick them up and put them back (or allow them to stay – your choice!). Don't engage in conversation and chances are they'll soon decide they're probably better off in their own bed.

> 'My mother told me that most things with children are phases and just about as soon as you think you can stand it no longer it changes. Don't fret!' (susiecb)

SHOULD SMALL CHILDREN EAT MEALS AT THE TABLE?

Consensus – absolutely yes! Eating in front of the telly (or with other distractions) can mean:

> 'That you eat just to shovel in fuel rather than as a specific and enjoyable activity, and so quickly learn to

> ignore the signals that say your tummy is full. That's one of the reasons why obesity is an increasing problem in Western society.' **(absent)**

As well as ending up with (probably) less mess and (certainly) better digestion:

> 'The family table is where children learn a lot of their good manners and social skills, and you can't start too early. It might be a battle royal until she gets the message, but she'll thank you for it in later life.' **(artygran)**

WHO RULES THE ROOST?

Consensus – the grown-up. Always. Consistency is key. You don't want the child to end up confused by half-rules and moving goalposts. They need to know who's boss.

> 'Toddlers need boundaries, not choices. They are far too young to be making decisions for themselves. I once read that modern parents need to realise that as a parent they are in charge of what goes on in the child's life: they are not the child's entertainment director.' **(joan)**

If you make a threat in order to get a mutinous child to do something – for example: 'If you don't get in the buggy right now, then we won't be able to go to the park' – make sure you follow it through.

> 'If you promise a child a present, you make sure it arrives. If you say something will not happen, then you have to hold to that too, and not change your mind when they wear you down. If they learn young that eventually they always get their own way, however inconvenient it is to everyone else, they will never grow out of it – just grow up into an overbearing, selfish adult.' **(elegran)**

Not yet having the ability to communicate fully can make small children grumpy and frustrated. Tantrums and tears are a normal part of toddler behaviour; they're not called the terrible twos for nothing. Just hold on to the fact that, if only by virtue of your age and experience, anything they can do, you can do better – and that includes saying *no*!

> 'We are now confident people. We know much more than we did when we were young anxious parents, desperate to do all the right stuff, having read the books and got masses of conflicting advice from an array of "experts", friends and family. So confusing! Getting the balance is hugely difficult and that is where we grandparents come into our own, providing a relaxing place where any antisocial behaviour can be quietly ignored and then we move on to something better.' **(elizabethjoan)**

Praising the good rather than criticising the bad can also reap rewards:

> 'The best piece of advice I ever had was to "Catch my child being good". Some children get more attention when they are behaving in a challenging way than when they are being quiet and compliant. If they behave well, even for a few seconds, then the praise should kick in immediately.' (toria100)

If you pigeonhole a child as 'the naughty one', 'the cheeky one' or 'the difficult one', chances are they will grow into their label. By offering praise when it's deserved you are providing an incentive to improve.

And when they are having 'a moment'? As long as they're not a danger to themselves or anyone else, take a deep breath, smile sweetly and ignore it. As the old saying goes: 'No audience, no performance'. And who knows better than we do that the old ones are very often the best?

> 'My nearly-four granddaughter is very keen to have a sleepover with us. We were visiting a few weeks ago and she decided to scream at the top of her voice because we were paying more attention to her baby sister. When her mum told her that Grandma and Granddad wouldn't want to have her to stay if she behaved like that, she witheringly replied, "Well, I wouldn't be naughty at

THEIR house, would I?" Such killer logic and completely unanswerable, especially when you are trying to keep a straight face!' (gulligranny)

HEALTH

Babies and toddlers may be charming, adorable and the best things since sliced bread, but they are also germ magnets. And what they get they tend to spread.

'Dear little children do get extra cuddly when they are under the weather and wipe their snot around everywhere. Cold viruses are for sharing ... Most important is to keep washing your hands thoroughly and often and try to avoid touching your face. Most cold viruses don't infect by droplets, they infect by hand to eye or hand to nose. So if the grandchild is snotty, avoid nuzzling and kissing her too. (Hard, I know, as they are lovely even if snotty.)' (JessM)

Other than hygiene, tips for avoiding the bugs (which, alas, are often unavoidable nonetheless) are a balanced diet with plenty of fruit and veg, a decent amount of sleep, plus moderate exercise and lots of fresh air.

POTTY-TRAINING

How long does it take to toilet-train a small child? The honest answer is, how long is a piece of string? Some take to it like a duck to water. Others … don't.

It's perfectly possible to be a gran now and to have brought up your own children in the era of disposable nappies. But others of us hail from the days before disposables (or perhaps have heard tell of these strange ways from our mothers), when the aim was to get children potty-trained *as soon as possible*. That was the thinking, in fact, for hundreds of years. If you think about getting through half a dozen terry nappies a day without the benefit of a washing machine, you can see why.

Those of us who can remember back to the Pleistocene era of dangling your child over the potty from the age of about six weeks (it worked, honestly!) may be sceptical about the current disapproval of early potty-training. They may think it's, well, odd, that as soon as there was serious money in nappies, conventional wisdom became that children should no longer be dry during the day within a year but should take their own time. Involving the parents, of course, in buying those nappies for years.

But that's the way it is. Having lived through both eras (some of us are immensely old and have had a lot of children over a long time) we can safely say that new parents are unlikely to want to be the weird ones with the eccentric potty-training habits that are widely viewed by society as psychologically damaging to infants. And, let's face it, none of us would want to go back to all that washing.

So these days you are likely to be potty-training a fairly rational and communicative child. Some children, consequently, react well to a chart with a reward, say, for getting to a certain number of stars. It doesn't have to be anything big or expensive. It's remarkable how a piece of plastic tat can be the most powerful incentive for a child who's set their heart on a particular little doll or a miniature car for example. This method also has the benefit of positive reinforcement: aka rewarding something done well. Others find that inducements such as sweets can do the trick.

> 'Bribery works like a charm. Ignore all the health visitors who say you shouldn't. Many children just need an incentive. I did this with all mine – they had one jelly tot or one dolly mixture if they did it in the right place – no problem! And sometimes if I could see they needed to go and they were putting it off I would say, "Let's go and choose which colour jelly tot you are going to have – sit on the pot and we can look through the packet." To those who were horrified I would say, "Don't worry, I am sure that they will have left off the jelly tot by the time they get married!"'
> (Mishap)

Lots of people favour setting aside a few days to make a concerted effort to get the whole thing done – a sort of potty boot camp if you will. If you're doing this in the summer, there are worse methods to try than the in-the-garden-with-no-nappy technique. Lawns are far better places to collect puddles than rugs or carpets and there's many a child who's found success this way. Boys are notorious for being more tricky than girls in the potty department, but the fact that they are better equipped to 'aim' means the whole outdoor 'watering the flowers' incentive can add a new dimension.

POTTY-TRAINING PROBLEMS

If a child is resisting the whole potty-training thing in order to retain control, let them see that it's not an issue for you. Clearly it *will* be an issue and may lead to many sleepless nights, but hide this – *well.* If they can see that their ploy is not working, then they'll eventually capitulate and find another way to drive you up the wall instead!

Many children have issues with 'number twos' and will continue to resist pooing on the loo long after they are dry. There can be a number of reasons for this, many of which boil down to fear. Some may have passed a hard stool and the pain has made them reluctant to go there again. For others, a loud 'splosh' associated with something coming out of their bodies is alarming (nappies, of course, cushion the sound).

'My second son was scared of falling down the loo. I remember (I must have been about that age) being scared I would go down the plughole of the bath when the plug was removed.' **(JessM)**

Some children simply find the very idea of using the loo a complete hassle. With disposable nappies drawing moisture away from small behinds, discomfort is no issue and they are perfectly happy to continue as they are. Some gransnetters have found going back to terries helpful during training. There's nothing like a cold, damp heft of towelling to help you understand the joy of a nice clean pair of pants.

If that doesn't work, we have one further suggestion for the very reluctant toddler. You might not want a little visitor scrutinising your every move(ment) when you're in the smallest room yourself, but leading by example can really work and help to demystify the whole process.

'We used to have "inspections" as to who could do the biggest wee, etc. Sounds very funny when I write all this down but it all seemed very natural at the time. Must have passed this on to the grandchildren as well because they delight in letting you inspect their outputs – my husband thinks it is "awful" – but it does mean that they think of their toilet visits as something very healthy and not to be frightened about!' **(MDougall)**

MONEY AND GIFTS

SAVING FOR GRANDCHILDREN

> 'I opened accounts for each of my grandchildren which need my signature should they need to withdraw money. Not applicable yet as they are all very young.' (sook)

It's something that most of us would like to do, but many of us simply aren't in a position to. If you're not, the simple rule is don't even think about it. And, even if you are, there are plenty of things to think about before you go ahead.

For example, it's important to consider whether other grandchildren might come along at some point. It's hard (and the stuff of family feuds) if you're not able to treat them equally. While you might find it reasonably easy to put money away for one or two, that's very different to suddenly having to find funds for six or seven.

> 'When our first grandchild was born I bought Premium Bonds in her name and on her first and subsequent birthdays we gave her a cheque to bank. When the second was born I did the same. I don't think there will be any more grandchildren so my finances will allow me to maintain what I have started.' (harrigran)

If you are able to afford to do something at the moment, do consider what your own needs might be in the future before making a long-term commitment.

Many people who are in a position to save for their grandchildren find adding to the fund on birthdays and at Christmas can be more manageable than, say, a monthly direct debit. Don't forget that even small amounts will add up over a long period and – in these days of tuition fees, unemployment and soaring house prices – they can really make an enormous difference to a young adult who is off to university, trying to find a job or attempting to get a foot on the housing ladder.

How Best to Put Money Aside?

Most banks offer savings accounts especially for children so it's always worth looking into what's currently on offer.

If your grandchild was born before 2011, they will have a Child Trust Fund (CTF). Even though this long-term tax-free savings plan has now been scrapped, you can still pay into existing accounts. These can be topped up by a maximum of £1,200 a year until the child turns 18.

If they don't have a CTF, other options for tax-free saving include:

- Tax Exempt Savings Plans (TESPs)
- Junior ISAs
- Children's Bonus Bonds (from National Savings and Investments).

With the first two options the funds can't be touched until your grandchild reaches the age of 18. There's an annual maximum that can be added, so don't forget to check whether the parents have any plans in place themselves as this could impact on how much you can put away for a child.

Bonus Bonds can be opened by an adult for any child under 16 and earn annual interest as well as bonuses every five years until the child is 21. The bonds are under parental control until the child turns 16, after which point they are able to take control themselves. If you'd prefer them to be a little older before they get to lay their hands on any savings, this might not be the right route for you.

Do remember that, while there's a whole range of options, rates and savings plans change all the time and it's always worth going through what's available with your bank, building society or financial adviser to make sure that you've found the one that suits you best.

> 'I am thinking of leaving my grandchildren a percentage in my will to be shared out between them at my demise. My children think it a good idea but don't seem to understand that the money will have to be held in trust and someone will have to look after this – and I'm not too sure of the long-term implications.' **(heleena)**

Legacies are, of course, another option to think about, although it's definitely worth getting professional advice to consider any tax or administrative implications before changing your will to accommodate your wishes.

OTHER PRESENTS FOR GRANDCHILDREN

Giving gifts – even non-financial ones – is an issue that can prove surprisingly thorny and that throws up a number of questions such as:

- How much should you spend?
- Should you ask your grandchild (or their parents) what they want first or buy what you like?
- Do you have to spend the same amount on each grandchild?
- What if they don't like what you've bought?
- Do you do anything if you discover your gifts have been returned or exchanged?

> 'I hate to say it but my son and daughter-in-law are a bit snobbish and have returned some of the outfits I have bought for the baby because they don't like items with writing or characters on or they have been bought from supermarkets! They seem to expect clothes from exclusive boutiques, which is a joke as we are on a debt-management plan!' **(happygran1964)**

The golden rule above all others is: don't buy anything that you can't afford. Never feel bad if you don't have a lot to spend. We've found that one small, thoughtful gift can easily trump a whole bag of expensive presents when it's something that the child will really love. And big is not necessarily better.

> 'Many grandparents buy expensive wooden toys when young children actually prefer brightly coloured plastic. And I have never known a baby who could play with a three-foot high teddy bear.' (greatnan)

However much you are spending, it's probably a good idea to run your plans past the parents first – if only to make sure that you are not buying duplicate gifts.

> 'I always ask my daughters-in-law for ideas for presents. One of them is brilliant with suggestions, often giving me an eBay link. And what I buy for her son is often appropriate for the other two as well. All too soon they will reach the stage when only hard cash will do!' (annobel)

Of course if everyone *does* end up buying the child a princess dress or a policeman's helmet or a pair of *Peppa Pig* pyjamas then, clearly, some things will have to go back to be exchanged for something else. But if your gift choice is rejected simply because they don't like it, it can be very hurtful. If you do discover the hard way that your taste in clothes is very different to theirs, it might be easier to stick to books or toys in future, unless you are happy to acknowledge that what you have chosen might well be taken back.

'I always buy Next or M&S with a gift receipt for here, and only sales clothes for my two grandchildren abroad. Then I don't care what happens. My son-in-law abroad always washed clothes on a very hot cycle which ruined most things as he never really liked anything I bought, but now he has realised that children will wear what they want and quite often they look as though no one cares – so is grateful for M&S input.' **(stansgran)**

It's also worth remembering that, while your own children may have been kitted out in head-to-toe hand-knit in infancy, the trend for woollen leggings and matinee jackets is well and truly over.

Do check before slogging over the knitting needles into the wee small hours. It's one thing having something you've bought shoved into the back of a drawer, never again to see the light of day, but if it's something you've made from scratch it can be devastating to see all that effort go to waste.

'I think all grandmas want to knit something for their new grandchild, don't they? And we all have the feeling that we'll be unlikely to see the baby wearing it, especially after the first week or so.' **(greenmossgiel)**

That's not to say a handmade present will go unappreciated. A cardi or sweater might very well be received with enthusiasm, and lots of new mums would be only too delighted to receive one as a gift.

> 'My daughter in Sydney has asked me to look out for some baby cardigans for her next soon-to-be-born baby, "You know, Mum, the sort of cardis that little old ladies knit!" I have been lurking in all the charity shops, but no luck so far. I would knit one myself, but as I am still on the one I started for her first baby eight years ago, I don't think there's much chance of me finishing it this time round.' (gally)

Even if your gifts go down a treat, do shop wisely and be aware that whatever you choose may come back to haunt you.

> 'My son and daughter-in-law are very nice about anything we get for the grandsons but, funnily enough, the toys that make loud noises and the drums, tambourines and whistles always seem to end up at our house for them to play with when they are here.' (Lilygran)

However much you enjoy giving, when you have a number of children, children-in-law and grandchildren, Christmas and birthdays can suddenly get very expensive. If buying gifts for everyone is too much or beyond your budget, why not consider the following:

- Agree within the family that you will only buy presents for children and not for adults.
- Create a limit for adult presents so it doesn't get out of hand. This can work surprisingly well. It's amazing what you can get for, say, £10, and trying to be clever and resourceful can actually make shopping more fun.
- Come up with a Secret Santa arrangement for the adults. Agree a budget. If you only have to buy for one person, it often means it can be a little higher than if you were buying for everyone. Put the participants' names in a hat, pick one each and buy a present for that person. Obviously you don't have to keep who you are buying for a secret, but it can certainly add to the fun.
- Have a cut-off point where you stop buying gifts, instead of continuing ad infinitum.

'My four siblings and I, plus the various daughters- and sons-in-law, agreed what Mum called a "non-aggression" pact as well – we don't exchange presents at Christmas. Some years ago I also told my mum not to worry about sending me a birthday gift but to give something to her favourite charity instead, if she felt like it.' **(baggy)**

'We have 17 grandchildren between us. Four over the age of 18, which is when we stop giving Christmas presents. I try to budget at £20 per child. As some reach the age of 18, another one is born, recent one three weeks ago. This is not the end of it though; our children also expect a present! It is really difficult to know how to stop this treadmill.' (Hattie64)

If you have a number of grandchildren, you might agree to set a limit on their Christmas and birthday gifts. It's perfectly reasonable to do so – especially if you are retired on a low income – and helps keep things fair. But, if the ages and requirements of each child are very different, you may prefer to keep it on a case-by-case basis.

'If I know that one of my children or grandchildren wants something particular that they are likely to make good use of, I will spend more. I gave up trying to be "fair" (if you define that as spending the same on everyone) when my children were small – I reckon it all evens out in the end.' (PatriciaPT)

And talking of the season of goodwill …

DO YOU BELIEVE?

'I always explain the Father Christmas thingy away as it's magic in a hushed whisper, meant to convey that we are not supposed to understand the how, just enjoy it!' (susiecb)

For those who celebrate Christmas, one of the nicest things to do when small children are around is to leave things out for Santa and share the wee ones' incredulity (well-faked, of course) when you discover that he's 'actually' eaten all the mince pies and Rudolph has polished off his carrots to boot.

Clearly if you have a chimney this makes things a lot easier. If you don't, then a little ingenuity may be called for. Think ... keys? Magic? Tiny elves?

> 'I think it is good to have a little magic in their lives, it soon passes and reality hits them all too soon. I don't feel bad about these kind of "lies", we are keeping the magic alive for a while.' (GoldenGran)

Some plump for a more logical approach.

> 'I never lie to the grandchildren. If asked, I explain that Santa Claus is mythological, same as Dr Who, Robin Hood, Cinderella and (dare I say it?) Jesus. I reckon that once they are old enough to understand what mythological means they are old enough to know.' (Granny23)

The age at which you can expect children to stop believing in Santa varies (factors definitely include whether or not there are older siblings on the scene), but the consensus is generally somewhere around seven or eight.

A word of warning: once they do come to terms with the discovery, you need to remind them not to spread the word to small brothers and sisters and friends.

'I think my eldest daughter was around 10 years old or possibly older ... when I told her that the tooth fairy didn't exist. She told me that I had ruined all of her fantasies.' (faye)

That said, how long do you really want it to go on?

'Where did we go wrong? Until two years ago my husband was staying up way past midnight to tiptoe into kids' (30, 28, 26, 22) bedrooms to hang up stockings and drink the sherry ... I tried many times to tell him they had guessed it was him and not Santa! Thankfully both sons got married last year and now have their own Christmas Eve!' (grannylin)

'My children aged 50, 48 and 40 years all still believe in Father Christmas! When they were young we told them that if they didn't believe he would not come, so, of course, they still believe. Father Christmas comes every Xmas Eve and leaves them each a present – this is in addition to their regular present, of course. Who is the idiot in the family?' (riclorian)

CHAPTER SIX
BIGGER GRANDCHILDREN

'I'm feeling quite proud of myself. While his parents can only get grunts or shrugs out of my teenage grandson, I managed to get a "whatever" yesterday.' (libertybodice)

There's an old saying: 'Small children, small problems, bigger children, bigger problems'. And it's oh so true. Although little ones can be utterly exhausting, the majority of issues you are likely to face are practical ones, such as chronic lack of sleep, working out how to remove a toddler having a tantrum from the bread aisle at Tesco or how best to get the smell of wee out of your favourite sandals when potty-training goes wrong. But as children get older, start school and begin making their way in the big wide world, outside influences begin to creep in and suddenly you can find yourself back at the sleepless-night stage, lying awake and worrying about everything from Internet safety to exam results, first love to eating disorders.

MODERN TECHNOLOGY

You may have survived the school days and teenage years with your own kids, but that was likely in the days before social media, online chat rooms, 24-hour telly, mobile phones and the rest. While it's true that modern technology brings with it many benefits (not least Gransnet!), it also throws up an entirely new set of problems that you probably won't have had to face before.

HOW MUCH SCREEN TIME IS TOO MUCH SCREEN TIME?

> 'I remember my mother telling me I'd get square eyes if I saw *Watch with Mother* more than twice in a week. Heaven knows what's going to happen to my grandchildren who seem to spend half their lives in front of the telly.' (chunkalunka)

That brief 15-minutes-a-day window for children's TV has long since been replaced with channels galore, providing programmes specifically for teens, tweens, toddlers and tiddlers 24/7. And that's before we even get started on DVDs and videos and hard-drive recorders and Internet downloads. Frankly, it's a miracle we can tear the little darlings away.

How much is too much is a bit like asking how long a piece of string is, especially when one news report will blame all of society's evils on sticking children in front of the small screen, while another will say it doesn't do them the slightest bit of harm.

Whichever side you and their parents come down on, the fact is that there are some great programmes around these days, many of which have educational benefits too. And not just for kids – we would know absolutely nothing about vast areas of the globe without David Attenborough.

But, of course, in this day and age there's more to screens than just the telly. With laptops, PCs, iPads, mobiles, computer games ... sometimes your average living room can feel more like a branch of Currys than a family chill space.

Only recently there have been reports about the rise in the number of children who are hooked on using smartphones and tablets. One four-year-old was sent for psychiatric treatment after becoming Britain's youngest known iPad addict and many other pint-sized patients have displayed compulsive behaviour after using these devices from a very early age.

Now clearly these are extreme examples, but they do illustrate the fact that parents (and, of course, grandparents) are right to limit the time that children spend on computers, games and the like.

Of course it's great to pick up technological skills early and it's tough to be the only one in the playground who hasn't seen the latest episode of whatever the cool programme happens to be this week. But stick with the old adage of moderation in all things and you'll be doing them a favour (they won't necessarily agree!).

There are many reasons why limiting screen time (of any type) is important. Using time away from techy pursuits to develop the imagination, creative skills, social interaction, enjoy sport and good old-fashioned fresh air is vital for youngsters of any age. Plus it's not good for anyone's eyesight – or general health – to spend hour after hour hunched over a screen in a darkened room.

All the same, technology is an important part of life for most of us. Learning and communication have been revolutionised by computers and embracing that can bring benefits for all.

> 'There is a big World Wide Web out there and the Internet is probably the best educational tool ever invented ... and some of us on Gransnet probably spend just as many of our waking hours on the laptop as any 12-year-old.' **(helshea)**

Even if you are finding it impossible to prise teens from their screens, do try not to panic.

'My son had a similar habit. Now he is a senior systems analyst in the USA at only 24 years of age. He loves every minute he is at work and has now returned to physical activity when he is not at work.' **(J13)**

ONLINE SAFETY

There's lots of amazing and appropriate stuff for children on the Web, but there's lots of not-so-savoury and inappropriate stuff out there too. Sometimes children may come across this inadvertently:

'Dear English teacher, when you set 13-year-old boys homework which includes asking them to explain the phrase "down-going men" (from *Jekyll and Hyde*), you should think about what a Google search will produce.' **(Keren)**

Sometimes they may come across things during a, well, let's say a 'purposeful' search – something particularly common with teenage boys. So how best to make sure they use the Internet safely? It's easier, of course, with younger children, at least most of the time:

'I googled "clown fish" for my four-year-old grandson and one of the options was "have sex with a clown fish". I really had thought this was a pretty safe search!' **(Mishap)**

For starters it's always a good idea to make sure that they use the computer in the same room as an adult rather than in their bedroom – and, on this front, pre-teens are far more likely to comply. Helping them with homework and other projects can not only avoid any problems, but can also be (surprisingly) enjoyable for you both.

With older children, who are less likely to be under your watchful eye all the time, it's important to educate them about online safety. Emphasise that the Web has both positives and negatives, but do so without scaring them (nightmares about online predators are definitely to be avoided) and without making your boundaries seem unreasonably strict (forbidden fruit is, after all, always the most tempting).

Treating them as young adults and sharing your concerns (for example, the dangers of chat rooms, fraud, viruses, online gambling and the like) and discussing how best to deal with them is likely to be far more productive than blanket bans and screaming rows.

While it's always advisable to keep tabs on any youngster's browsing habits in person, you may want to activate the parental control software on your devices. The software (which, crucially, is easy to switch on) can block content you'd like them to avoid and keeps records both of what's been viewed and what's been vetoed.

There are many safety controls available, but what they can do and how well they can do it can vary enormously so it's always best to get expert advice (not least because, like any software, there are updates all the time).

As with all media (everything, really), the most important things are giving the children a confident sense of themselves and the ability to make critical judgements. So talking to them about television programmes or books you share when they're younger will help them to work out what's genuine or dangerous on the Internet when they're older and on their own.

SOCIAL MEDIA

Yes, you are meant to be at least 13 before you sign up to Facebook, but this doesn't stop many younger children opening their own accounts simply by faking their date of birth (and no, no one checks). There is no minimum age on Twitter. And, rather inevitably, along with this accessibility comes a certain degree of risk.

Although social networks can be fun and even a power for good (many a Facebook or Twitter campaign has achieved great things), it goes without saying that, just like anywhere else on the Web, there can be people whose intentions are not entirely honourable (be they to open vulnerable young minds to extreme or distasteful views or to engage in abusive or illegal activity). It must be stressed these make up only a tiny minority of users, but online safety is paramount for anyone (of any age) using networks that can be accessible to friends and strangers alike.

Before joining any social networking site it's important to make sure that children fully understand the concept of digital privacy – or lack of it. For example:

- Unless you sign up to 'protect' your tweets (which means that only people you allow into your network can read them) anyone anywhere in the world will be able to see them. Clearly if you are tweeting that you are eating a cheese sandwich in front of the telly this isn't going to do anyone any harm. But it's amazing how much people can reveal – in just 140 characters – that can seriously jeopardise personal safety and reputation.
- The fact is that if you tweet that you are off on holiday for a week, then it's an open invitation to a burglar to come ransack your empty house. And, yes, this happens. A lot. It's generally not that tricky to work out where someone lives once you know their name and have access to their tweets.
- We've all read newspaper reports of teens who've decided to have a few friends over, posted this on Facebook or twitter and suddenly found themselves with a house full of uninvited strangers and thousands of pounds' worth of damage. Children need to understand how easy it is for a casual invitation to a couple of mates to go viral and spiral completely out of control.
- If a child tweets that they have copied someone else's homework or cheated in an exam, there is every

chance that a parent, teacher or a classmate will see that information and act on it (again, this is not uncommon). There's a fine line, though. Classmates often set up homework help pages to share information on what's been set and to collaborate and help each other, which can be incredibly useful (not least when they get on to differential calculus, where we're afraid we just don't have much to offer).

- Universities and employers can also unearth information with surprising ease. The impact of one's digital footprint should never be forgotten.
- If youngsters are tweeting about where they and their friends are meeting up, they should remember that anyone can see that information and turn up too (with enough details about friends, family, etc. from other tweets to get them to drop their defences).
- Nowhere is peer pressure more apparent than on social media. Cyber bullying is something we could never have dreamed of when our own children were young, but it is something to be only too aware of today. The fact is that it's much easier to say nasty things about someone online than it is face-to-face, but it is absolutely no easier to deal with the pain that this may cause.
- Sexting too is scarily common. We heard a joke the other day that went something like: 'You meet someone, fancy them, flirt a bit and then send them a picture of your breasts.' No, well, perhaps it isn't

all that funny, but you'd be amazed how much of it goes on. It's as well to remind kids that these things can fall into the wrong hands. Without being alarmist, blackmail over pictures is one of the ways that predators exploit young people and up the ante, getting them to send more explicit images. Much illegal material these days is – worryingly – generated by young people themselves.

Even if you do allow a child to use Twitter on the proviso that their tweets are protected, it's still worth regular checks on who they have allowed into their network.

Likewise, Facebook. If a child is underage, it's often a good idea to make it a condition of use that they allow a parent or grandparent to be a 'friend' and therefore able to keep an eye on what they're up to. Schoolchildren seem to be able to build staggeringly large networks in the blink of an eye, suddenly ending up with 500 'friends' or more. But they need to understand that these will include people that they really don't know very well and therefore it's important to think carefully about what they're posting (which inevitably they don't).

'I had to have a very stern talk with my 12-year-old grandson about privacy settings and swearing on Facebook. You are broadcasting, basically. On the one hand, it's great to see that he is technologically adept – on the other, neither he nor his friends seem to spare a

> second to think about their online reputation. But, once it's out there, it's out there for all eternity. I feel sorry for them in a way. I can't imagine the awful things I was saying at that age (e.g. my crush on Illya Kuryakin from *The Man from U.N.C.L.E.*) hanging around for posterity. Cringe.' **(sneetch)**

The latest thing is teen flirting sites. These are both anonymous and open, so look safe, however, it is also often possible to get into one-to-one conversations. Much of what goes on on these sites is innocent enough and, in the case of gay teenagers, for example, their existence can lead to a much happier, less isolated adolescence. But the problem with anonymity is you just don't know who you're talking to.

You can see the problem ...

It's a case of giving your grandchildren the resilience and critical ability to differentiate something a bit fishy from something that's simply fun and also the confidence to speak to an adult if they feel they may be getting out of their depth. This is something that has to start *before* they actually hit the age when they'll be using these sites.

We don't know a teen who isn't involved in social media in some sense, and we're the last people to think that that's necessarily a bad thing, because we love social media and know how many pleasures and benefits it can bring. By talking to them about the sites they like, what they get out of them and what *they* see as the hazards (you may be pleasantly surprised by how informed they are!) you are far more likely to be able to equip a child to be able to make informed and sensible decisions.

GAMING

We have particularly fond memories of our first experience of 'video' gaming – that black screen with two white dashes and a dot and the many (many) happy hours playing 'tennis' and believing ourselves to be at the cutting edge of technology.

Even if we haven't become vastly more sophisticated, the games that are available have. Now simply plugging in a console can take you to complex and frighteningly realistic new worlds in glorious technicolour. (Bring back the dots!)

Games – like films – come with guide certification, but it can be hard to limit age-appropriate access when children have older siblings or are playing at the homes of friends whose parents take a more cavalier attitude.

> 'Some people seem to think of the games like cartoons – i.e. not really problematic – but I worry that they can make children think that violence and aggression are normal. Saying that, neither my grandson nor his friends seem to be remotely violent despite their addictions to *Call of Duty*. I hope we have managed to instil in them that violence is not a way to solve things in real life. On

> the plus side, the games flatter their quick reactions (unlike mine) and they all have very strong thumbs!' (eggmayo)

This is another area where we have found talking really helps. Listening to them explaining what they get out of the games is often illuminating. They can be surprisingly articulate about the graphics and the storylines, the skills the games test and the rewards they offer (and if you are used to them communicating in grunts, this can make a pleasant change).

Ask them to show you what's going on. Talk about anything you find disturbing about the content – and you can always resort to the it's-all-too-much-for-gran wilt to show them that you don't entirely approve of the violence and get them to explain why *they* think it's not harmful.

When it comes to censorship, you're only going to be as effective as the least monitored child in their group of friends. In other words, you may not be able to stop them playing violent games at other people's houses, even if you can ban them at yours. So better, on the whole, for them to know *what* it is you don't like about these games (and it's not enough to say you've heard they're bad for you – you probably, unfortunately, need to find out for yourself). If they can talk sensibly about the games and about your fears, they're well on the way to seeing them *as* games, rather than as a blueprint for life.

*

As we've said before, technology in all forms is part of a child's education and preparation for the world. Nonetheless, it's important not to let it take over. Getting them off the PlayStation/Xbox/computer to focus on homework or simply be part of the family can be difficult, but it's important enough to be worth the battle.

PHONES

Obviously Internet access and gaming are no longer restricted to PCs and laptops (it is good to know that parental control software is available for mobiles too). But do children actually need phones in the first place? And if they do, from what age is it acceptable to have one?

The bottom line is: however much they may try to persuade you otherwise, no child needs a phone until they have a degree of independence and may need it to contact you if problems arise. For example, if they start to walk or take the bus to school on their own (or with friends) rather than with an adult, a phone is useful both for emergencies or for keeping tabs.

Clearly if this is the purpose of any phone you might buy, then it doesn't matter how basic the model might be. It is almost inevitable that the youngster in question will not agree: 'But *eeeverybody's* got a smartphone!' Are you being mean to stick to your guns or to encourage the parents to do the same?

> 'BlackBerries are for harassed executives who need to access their emails around the clock. Eleven-year-olds do not need constant access to emails or the Internet. Why would you want one unless you have to have one? They are expensive ... Give in on this one and they will want an upgrade next year!' (JessM)

We will take that as a 'no' then.

KEEPING THEM OCCUPIED

So, what to do with them when we've prised them away from the computer? Times have changed, whether we like it or not (and we're not always sure we do), and, for many people, gone are the days of packing kids off on their bikes for the day with nothing more than a sandwich and a warning not to be late home for tea.

While many parents – and grandparents – would no longer dream of letting kids roam fields and forests on their own, it is, of course, important to find a balance between being overprotective and still allowing children to enjoy some freedom and to experience important rites of passage.

Perhaps one of the biggest moments of childhood is deciding when to let them go to the local shop by themselves – chewing your nails till they come back, perfectly happy, of course, and usually having remembered to pick up whatever spurious item you'd asked them to get in the first place.

It's only natural to worry about stranger danger, despite the fact that the publicity generated by what are rare but appalling cases definitely gives us a distorted view of how prevalent this is. So how do you explain personal safety to a child without scaring them too much to ever leave your side?

> 'Having been a child at the time of the Moors murders, I was told about not getting into cars with people and, sensitive soul that I was, had nightmares abut this for years. I avoided giving my own children the sense that people were out to get them. I wanted them not to be frightened of the world. But you have to make clear that children must always tell you where they're going. You can make this a rule without being alarmist about it. Phones make this a bit easier once they're old enough to have them.' **(givemehrt)**

PRE-TEENS

Obviously factors such as where you live, the age and personality of the child, what's available locally and how much time (or cash) you can spend will have a bearing on what you might end up doing, but finding age-appropriate activities doesn't have to be a Herculean task in itself.

Children of primary-school age and older often enjoy cooking and baking, especially since TV programmes like *The Great British Bake Off* made it cool. They can take on more responsibility than little ones (you're probably not going to have a heart attack if you spot them with a knife in hand. Probably ...), but obviously it's still important that you are helping and supervising. They can make stuff for the family or try their hand at more sophisticated decorating, icing and the like than little ones.

If you have a garden, then energetic children can be a delight to share the joys of the outdoors with. If you've got a spare bit of flower bed or space for a growbag or large pot, why not turn it over to them as a mini allotment? There's no age barrier on being able to grow your own and not much beats the satisfaction of harvesting and munching on fruit and veg that you've grown from seed yourself.

Pond dipping or rock pooling is always a winner, although clearly you need a pond or a rock pool within reachable distance to make it work. Spare socks and shoes can prove to be extremely useful.

This suggestions sounds ridiculously simple, but if your grandchildren never go on trains or buses, then why not go on a train or bus? It can be a real treat. If they're into planes and you live near an airport, you can do worse than heading off to sit under the flight path with a picnic.

'I used to take my son on the bus into Manchester to see the huge snakes (live ones) in the museum and then we used to go to a cafe. I also took an eight-year-old boy to the garden centre and looked at the tropical fish. I let him use a digital camera and take lots of photos.' (JessM)

One money-saving tip: if you are planning on days out with any children over five, consider investing in a Family & Friends Railcard for substantial discounts on fares. They often pay for themselves the first time you use them.

Many children are happy kicking a ball around in the garden or park for hours on end. Frisbees can be a hit too, as can building dens (indoors or out) or putting up tents. Indeed, if the weather (and the garden/your nerves) are up to it, why not build a campfire and cook bangers or toast marshmallows?

Card games are easily adapted to a child's age, and other games – Monopoly, Operation, Junior Scrabble, Mouse Trap (all the old favourites) can go down a treat too. If you no longer have your original sets, it's often easy to pick up a bargain in an online auction.

'When my grandson was seven and eight he loved games like dominoes, draughts and chess as he gradually learned strategy and would whoop with delight when he outwitted me. I have no need to pretend to lose to him – it takes all my skill to win at these games now. It's a great way to be able to sit and chat too, without them feeling they are being interrogated by grandmother.

Even asking "Do you want gravy with this?" becomes the Spanish Inquisition from that age. Now we're getting the occasional "Uggh", which can mean "Yes", "No", "I don't mind" or "Stop asking me questions".' (carol)

Other activities that have gone down well with gransnetters' small fry include modelling clay, treasure hunts and matchbox challenges (where you pack as many small objects into a matchbox as you can – try theming it too).

If you're looking after the children for a few days (or longer), don't think that every day has to involve a major excursion. Many children are happy just to potter, and it's important to build in some time for relaxation (for them as well as you) too. Whether it's curling up companionably with books or enjoying a film on the telly, it's time that you will both treasure.

HOW TO HELP GRANDCHILDREN GAIN CONFIDENCE

Keeping them busy is one thing – making sure they're happy can be quite another. Many children go through a wobble of confidence at some point and granny's support can often be a big help in getting through difficult times.

Being there to listen can make a difference in itself; this is where it can really help to be one step – or generation – removed. Asking a child's opinion on things

– and listening to what they have to say – can be an enormous confidence booster. Whether the questions are daft or not, treat them respectfully and you'll have some fantastic conversations that can continue by phone, post or email if needed and make them feel like they really matter and are being taken seriously.

It's also worth remembering that many children like routine and knowing how things 'work'. Others find boundaries give them a feeling of security.

> 'I'll never forget one of my daughter's school friends saying, wistfully, "I wish we had rules like this in our house. It means you always know where you are."' (Marcella)

Giving children small, simple but 'vital' jobs can work a treat too. Put them in charge (the phrase matters!) of things like making sure you've locked the door when going out, or cleaning all the light switches and door handles, and remember to thank them for a job well done.

> 'When my daughter went to stay with her gran in the countryside, depending on the timing she would be responsible for planting/digging up potatoes, playing piano to make sure it was still in tune, etc. She knew she was genuinely being useful. We knew it wasn't the end of the world if she missed stuff. I have done the same with my own grandchildren.' (lottiee)

Praise achievement, but be encouraging when things don't go so well. It's amazing what a difference it can make to a child to know there's always someone batting for them. And there's nothing like positive reinforcement to help booster a fragile ego.

However, there's a balance to be struck between that kind of inner confidence and a sense of entitlement, and it can be tricky to find. Do stress the importance of politeness to everyone, to adults, of course, but also other children, and respect for other people's beliefs.

Family meals, parties and events can be tremendously important for children in giving them a sense of their own importance, but also reminding them that they are part of the whole and have to fit in. Grandparents can be *very* useful here. Above all, remember how old the child is and tailor your expectations accordingly.

> 'I'm still haunted by the fact I really lost it with my daughter one day and yelled at her, "Now you're just behaving like a baby". "I'm two," she replied ...' (gagaj)

SCHOOL

'My grandson has brought home some homework today. Venn diagrams. I had to ask him what they were and what we do with them. The thing is he seems to think

> I should already know and gets a bit agitated when I don't understand!' **(bikergran)**

Chances are that even if you did know what to do with them first time round you'll have long forgotten by now (that's our excuse anyway). But that's the wonder of the Internet – answers at your fingertips for pretty much every subject under the sun. This can be very useful as, if you're hoping to help and encourage, it's always good to know what you're talking about! And sometimes even small children's homework can seem fearfully complicated.

> 'And they say things are getting easier and standards are dropping! My daughter, when in the care of my mum, started talking about tessellations. My poor mum didn't know what she was on about and just said, "Sorry darling, I was away from school the day they taught that."' **(nanaej)**

EXAMS

One thing they never warned you about at school is that you don't have to be the one actually taking the exams to get stressed by them. We hate to be the ones to tell you, but if you found it hard work when your children were in the throes, don't think it gets any easier when it's grandchildren instead.

Now clearly we all want the ones we love to do as well as they possibly can, but how best to achieve this?

Recent research suggests that the same amount of revision spread out over time is better than cramming in the couple of days beforehand (not so surprising, really). Our tip is to work back from the exams to the point when they intend to start and factor in all the time they intend to take off – birthdays, hanging out with their friends – and build a timetable from there.

Fresh air and exercise are incredibly important when revising. The best method is 40 minutes of hard work, followed by 10 minutes of physical activity (running round the block, kicking a ball around in the back garden, etc.). More than four hours of revision a day is probably asking too much of anyone's brain. Plan treats so there's something to look forward to when they've done their quota for the day.

A question that has come up time and again on the forums is whether bribing for exam results is the way to go.

The consensus? A big fat no!

> 'I remember being offered a bicycle if I passed my 11+! I did, the bike was a second-hand nasty pale-blue job, bought from a neighbour. Bribes have a way of biting you on the backside.' **(amma)**

Now if other children are being offered, say, £100 per GCSE A grade (and it's not an uncommon scenario), your grandchild might feel a tad peeved that they're expected to put in the same level of effort for nothing more than a pat on the back. But it is best to stay firm and encourage them to work for the exams for what it will offer for their future.

> 'What's the going rate for A levels, first degree, master's degree? I want it – and the backlog of interest! Oh, for goodness' sake – GCSEs are not exactly major in the great scheme of things, but the benefit they have is all theirs, not yours.' **(absentgrana)**

It's invaluable for a child to know they have your support, though it is equally important for them to learn a sense of self-satisfaction from their own achievements.

Rewards are very different from bribery and some people do like to offer an incentive. We've found a small gift for working hard before the exams start can serve better in promoting the 'This is for doing your best' message than cash rewards for results.

> 'It worked for me and mine. Also don't harp on if the results are not brilliant. Be positive and work out a strategy for the future. Water under the bridge ... so move on.' **(Lynette)**

If a child has tried their best but not got the grades that they wanted or needed, be there to reassure them that it's not the end of the world, and tell them that sometimes things happen for a reason (hindsight is indeed a wonderful thing). There's many a person who's found themselves in a different career to the one they might have intended and odds-on this will turn out not to be so bad at all.

> 'My son got a bunch of Bs and Cs but is now a chiropractor and really likes it. He said the other day if he was suddenly rich he would want to carry on doing it. There is no way we could have guessed at 16 that this would be his chosen path in life.' (JessM)

DIFFICULTIES AT SCHOOL

One thing that hasn't changed – and likely never will – is that some children find school more of a challenge than others. Whether it's trouble making friends, not getting on with the teacher or struggling with the workload, having a sympathetic and supportive ear can make a world of difference.

Bullying

Of course there's a big difference between a simple spat and a prolonged campaign of bullying, which can take many forms, including: name-calling; teasing or humiliation; having money or possessions taken; being pushed, hit or hurt, being threatened; being ignored; or having rumours spread about you.

While many schools have programmes in place to deal with issues of this type, getting a child to admit there's a problem in the first place can be very difficult. The National Society for the Prevention of Cruelty to Children (NSPCC) has a list of signs to look out for if you are concerned that a child may be being bullied, which include:

- changes in mood or behaviour
- having trouble with schoolwork for no apparent reason
- using a different route home from school
- scratches or bruises
- clothes, possessions or money that have inexplicably disappeared or been damaged.

Even if a child does confide in you about a problem of this type, the odds are high that they will ask you not to tell anyone else. While speaking to the school – in confidence – is often the first step to tackle bullying, is it really your place to do so without the parents knowing what's happening?

> 'You do need to speak to them, but you shouldn't break the secret if he has asked you not to tell. Further discussion between you both first will hopefully get him to understand that he should speak to his parents about it. It needs careful handling. It's great that he feels

> he can talk to you and it would be a great pity if that trust was damaged in any way.' (phoenix)

Increased awareness about bullying means schools are far more clued-up about it than they have been before, and most will reinforce the message that it's vital to tell someone (be it a parent, grandparent or teacher) that it's happening.

It's absolutely natural that a child will be worried about repercussions, and this may well be the deciding factor in deciding to keep it to themselves. If you can't get them to open up about what's going on, make them aware that there are people they can speak to (confidentially) outside of family and school. Organisations such as ChildLine, Kidscape and Bullying UK are experts in the field and there to help children who feel that they can't confide in anyone they know, plus parents/grandparents who feel they are out of their depth when dealing with a situation.

It's important for children to understand that it is not their fault that they are being bullied and that most of us go (or have gone through) the experience of someone being mean to us. But keeping it a secret or hoping it will go away is never the best way to deal with it.

> 'We have a ground rule about secrets in our family – we don't keep them. We can keep quiet about nice surprises that will unfold in the next day or so, but

agreeing to keep secrets is a no-no. If a child asks me to keep one, I explain that I most likely won't be able to but they can safely disclose what they want to and I will do my best to ensure that they aren't blamed or harmed for sharing it with me. Adults take the responsibility for dealing with bullying, and children should be protected from retaliation.' **(whenim64)**

DYSLEXIA

Gone – fortunately – are the days when teachers pooh-poohed the very idea of dyslexia and even head teachers were sometimes heard to say that it was 'a middle-class excuse for less talented children'. That said, there's quite a lot of evidence to suggest that what diagnosis you get – dyslexia, dyspraxia, attention deficit hyperactivity disorder (ADHD) may depend partly on who is doing the diagnosing.

The fact is that the education system is quite rigid and pretty prescriptive. Children are expected to jump hurdles – SATs, GCSEs, AS and A levels, and all the various school tests and exams designed to prepare them for these – at particular points in their lives. But children's brains vary enormously. Some children are more distractable and less focused than others. For harassed teachers this may amount to 'Not concentrating in class' or 'Not keeping up', but those brains may well be doing all sorts of interesting things instead.

At least nowadays there are diagnoses to help explain why some children (quite a large number, in fact) don't conform to the timetable and shape of the education system. But those diagnoses are fairly blunt instruments and don't really explain the diversity and creativity of children's brains.

> 'In my first teaching job I had a class of reasonably bright children, one of whom simply could not spell. But dyslexia was not at that time in the teaching vocabulary. Many years later I remembered her and put two and two together. I often wonder what happened to her.' **(annodomini)**

Attitudes towards this – and other learning difficulties – have certainly changed enormously, and families struggling for years to convince the authorities that their children have a problem, or have been wrongly labelled 'slow' or 'rebellious', are (hopefully) becoming a thing of the past.

> 'My daughter suffered from dyslexia in spite of being highly intelligent. Unfortunately her comprehensive school failed to recognise it and she was put into the bottom stream, where she got bored and started being a nuisance. Three of her four children are also dyslexic, but they were luckier with their schools and had some one-to-one teaching. The Internet has been a boon too

– one granddaughter is studying for a degree with the OU [Open University] and finds spellcheck invaluable.' **(greatnan)**

These days there are many resources and strategies to help children with dyslexia and, with well-known people such as Richard Branson, Kirstie Allsopp, Bill Gates and Jamie Oliver all open about the fact that they are sufferers too, you can reassure your grandchildren that dyslexia is no longer a bar to doing anything that you want in life.

'It does make me angry that people don't realise that dyslexia has absolutely nothing to do with whether you are intelligent or not. In fact I read that 40% of millionaire businessmen are dyslexic, though only 10% of the general population.' **(broomsticks)**

Fortunately, by the time we become grans, most of us have known children who were mediocre at school yet turned into academically gifted students later in life. We'll have seen swotty, top-of-the-class children drop out or lose interest. And we'll know children who bumped along near the bottom at school who have become highly successful adults. Parents worry endlessly about school choices and exam results; grans know that these have a limited effect on what happens to you later in life. Which school you go to and how you fare there does affect your happiness in the short term, of course, but that's a slightly different matter.

SEX AND DRUGS AND ROCK 'N' ROLL

Between the rampant hormones and the pandemic of peer pressure, the teenage years can be tricky. There's something about hitting puberty that seems to render even the sweetest of children into a creature only able to communicate in unintelligible grunts. Thing is, having already survived and learned from this once before, grandparents are in pole position when it comes to translating the mumbles, grumbles and shoulder shrugs.

THE SEX BIT

By the time they reach their teens, most youngsters today know a great deal more about sex than we ever did at their age (and considerably older).

Go on – how many of us thought oral sex just meant talking about it? In our defence, we weren't the only ones with funny ideas.

> 'I was about 18 before I realised that people usually took their clothes off. Mum missed that bit out of her less-than-technical description. The only formal sex ed. I had was a cartoon which used aliens to show puberty.

> So if any do come to earth I'm an expert on that part of their development.' (vampirequeen)

Schools are better at educating about it, (most) parents are better at talking about it and the culture has changed so that the facts of life are (generally) no longer something gleaned from a pamphlet and never discussed again. And, of course, any confusion nowadays can usually be cleared up by a quick search on Google.

> 'I had a truly astonishing lack of information about sex. My convent education left me completely ignorant and there was no Internet to look at and no books available to me. I had been given such a hang-up about sex by the nuns that I didn't even like to talk about it with my girlfriends (who were probably as clueless as me). I certainly could not have asked my mother, who didn't even warn me about menstruation and never provided any sanitary towels.' (greatnan)

While it can only be a good thing to have moved on from the days where we were taught that sex was solely for procreation and never (ever!) for fun, there are fears that children now are growing up in such a sexualised atmosphere that sex is being foisted upon them before they can possibly have the faintest idea what it's all about. Even young kids are learning sexual terms from

TV, films and pop songs before they have a clue what any of them they really mean.

> 'One of my granddaughters (age seven) talks about being "sexy" and is desperate to have a boyfriend. I despair.' (specki4eyes)

However, all kids reach an age when they need to know about the mechanics, consequences and emotional implications of sex and relationships, and, as ever, education is key.

> 'The Netherlands has one of the most thorough sex-education programmes – and one of the lowest incidences of underage pregnancy. There is a lesson in there somewhere.' (greatnan)

Even if they're not having sex, there's every chance they might be looking at it. Thanks to the Internet, porn is more readily available than ever before and can offer impressionable young lads (and it is mainly though not exclusively boys) a hugely misleading idea of what sex is all about and what girls get out of it.

There is even evidence that college-age students are blaming some of their sexual dissatisfaction on porn, which emphasises power at the expense of intimacy, and the latest research shows that easy accessibility to this kind of adult material is something that really worries parents (and grandparents).

While our general mantra is that it's always good to be well-informed before tackling a tricky subject with a truculent teen, chances are that most grans really aren't going to want to look at porn and familiarise themselves with the ins and outs. As it were. So in this situation probably the best you can do is gently hint that pornography is actually a bit one-note and dull and doesn't begin to cover the range, quality, delight, surprise and pleasure of real-life sex.

THE DRINK BIT

> 'Drinking is a bit like smoking. All you can do is give a child the information about the harm these activities can cause and hope they'll take it on board eventually. Forbidding or condemning doesn't work.' **(Ana)**

Ain't that the thing?

Whatever you say or do, it's likely that most teenagers will experiment with alcohol at some point, and some will learn the hard way that too much is never a good thing.

Simply telling them to steer clear is unlikely to do the trick. Accepting that they probably will try and offering advice (rather than getting angry) are the words of wisdom from our forums. Perhaps use stories of any awkward situations caused by alcohol that you might have found yourself in at their age to illustrate the fact that most of us do stupid things at some point, but we (hopefully) grow out of it pretty quickly.

> 'And it's important to let them know that you don't need to drink to have a good time – and that being drunk can lead to really bad decision-making.' (susieb755)

Of course not all teenagers get drunk or have the desire to do so. But testing out alcohol is a pretty normal part of growing up. If they do take it too far, the important thing is that they learn from the experience.

> 'As a grandparent, I would be inclined to avoid rubbing salt into the wound – his (or her) parents will probably provide the "cross" factor. Disappointment, plus a gentle comment ... perhaps that most of us have done it at some point, but smart people learn the lesson ... will be far more effective than anger.' (inthefleld)

THE DRUGS BIT

Many – but not all – teenagers try drugs at some point – because they're 'Cool', because 'Everyone else is doing it', because they want to know what it feels like, because they're looking for an escape from stress or other problems, because they know it will wind you up. Or just to have fun ...

It's pretty easy to tell when a teenager has had too much to drink (the stumbling and whiff of vomit are usually a bit of giveaway), but with drugs it's not always so simple, especially when effects can vary from person to person.

> 'I have worked with teens and it can be very hard to tell. After all, some drugs make you energetic ... and some make you lethargic. Some affect speech, others don't. They may give you the munchies – or put you off food altogether. Youngsters taking drugs may become moody, start sleeping in all day and neglecting personal hygiene – but if you have ever lived with a teenage boy you'll know that that can be pretty much par for the course in any case. No – it's really not easy.' (minette)

Of course bigger behavioural changes will be more of a giveaway. If a teen suddenly becomes secretive, drops his friends without reason, starts missing school or exhibiting dramatic personality changes, something's going on and, yes, it could be drugs. If you do suspect they're using – or even dabbling – try to:

- Talk to them. Don't accuse or threaten, just listen to what they have to say and let them understand that they can trust you.
- Keep a close eye on what they're up to. If this means checking up on them, so be it.

- Stay calm and try to understand why they may be doing this in the first place.
- Find out more. You'll be in a better position to talk if you know what the drugs are and what they do. There is a great website called Frank (www.talktofrank.com), which is a mine of information. (Hands up who knew what bath salts were? And, no, we're not talking about crystals from Coty.) As its name suggests, it's, er, frank, which means that teenagers themselves like using it because it doesn't pussyfoot around the issues and isn't unnecessarily alarmist, but it makes clear that some substances, and some ways of using them, are dangerous.
- Get help. If you're out of your depth, there are plenty of people who can help and advise. Drugs services will offer your grandchild help at any stage, regardless of whether they're ready to change their behaviour. There are also support services, like Adfam, for families.
- Find out the facts. Don't lump soft drugs together with hard drugs. Your grandchildren will probably know more than you and will lose faith in what you're saying if you treat ecstasy and crack cocaine as basically the same or you use the slippery slope argument. (It's just not borne out by the facts.) But if you know your stuff, you'll be in a position to talk to them and they will respect what you say.

There is evidence that long-term use of cannabis can contribute to the development of psychotic illnesses in those who are predisposed. This is a serious issue – particularly, it seems, for boys – but that is not the same thing as an occasional puff on a joint at a party.

> 'I think all would-be cannabis users would benefit from spending a bit of time visiting the local psychiatric hospital. It's heartbreaking to hear story after story from parents and relatives of otherwise happy, bright young people whose lives have been turned upside down through the use of what used to be thought of as "soft" drugs. Some people are extremely lucky and get away with no ill effects, others have short-term paranoia and altered mind states – and then there are those who go on to develop long-term mental illness and whose lives are shot to pieces permanently.' (grannyactivist)

The most important thing is to talk to your grandchildren. Stay calm. Listen. And know how you'll react if they say they have tried drugs.

EATING DISORDERS

Some children will wolf down anything that's put in front of them. And others are, frankly ... a pain.

> 'Why does my grandson prefer pizza to ALL other foods? It's tiresome. What is it with kids and unhealthy eating?' (getmehrt)

But obviously, finicky faddiness (while irritating) is a world away from a life-threatening eating disorder. The fashion industry, airbrushing and the fixation with the 'perfect' size zero all contribute to unrealistic expectations of normal, healthy weight and mean that many young girls (and some boys – though mainly girls) become obsessed with being thin and doing anything they can to achieve it.

'Last week my granddaughter (four years two months) came home from preschool and when given her lunch had announced that she must not eat too much because otherwise she would not be thin when she was a grown-up lady. This in a home with no interest in celebrity culture and where there is no talk of diets, size or "good" and "bad" foods. My daughter-in-law said her blood ran cold when her daughter talked like that because the ideas could only have come from other children at preschool. Children she will be at school with next term and for at least the next six years.' (FlicketyB)

So what can be done to protect children from this pernicious obsession with being thin? Parents and grandparents doing all they can to put forward a sensible message is a start.

'Self-esteem was taught to me from my parents. I was short (still am!), a bit on the skinny side (no more!), with

> mousey, thin hair, but Mum and Dad made me feel like a princess. I have done my best with my three children and now my three grandchildren to make them feel good about themselves. Schools are there to teach all sorts of things, and I believe that parents can start the ball rolling at home with the right words. It's hard these days because the message out there is if you are beautiful you will go far, if not, well, no chance.'
> (Annika)

Eating disorders such as anorexia and bulimia are, of course, far more complex than a simple desire to be skinny: control, depression, insecurity and peer pressure can all play their part.

It can be difficult to go through adolescence as a girl nowadays. Expectations are incredibly high and often contradictory (girls are judged on their looks, but are also expected to achieve academically), and, to make matters worse, girls are still brought up to please other people. The effort to do so can be overwhelming at this time in their lives. (Wait till you become a gran, you want to say; it's fantastic, because you don't have to care any more!)

If boys tend to opt out by taking drugs, playing violent fantasy video games or perhaps looking at porn, girls in distress tend to turn inwards and do things that will punish themselves, such as eating disorders or self-harm.

An obsession with what you can or can't eat, distorted body image and an all-consuming preoccupation with weight are all symptoms of anorexia, yet many sufferers refuse to admit they have a problem and go to great lengths to disguise the extent of their illness.

So what signs should you look out for? An obsession with calories and fat and a refusal to eat 'bad' foods (such as carbs) despite having no need to lose any weight; a refusal to eat at mealtimes (often with excuses such as 'I've already eaten'); playing with/hiding food; and pretending to eat.

> 'I once worked on an eating-disorders ward, and we discovered that girls would store food in their cheeks then surreptitiously spit it into a vase of flowers that they'd "helpfully" offered to move.' (juno)

Other signs to watch out for are: baggy clothes used to hide a skeletal frame; an obsession with exercise; disappearing to the loo after meals to make themselves vomit (watch taps left running to mask the sounds); dramatic or extreme weight loss; a fixation on body image; and denial that there may be a problem.

If you do suspect that a grandchild has a problem, try to encourage them to seek professional help as soon as possible. As with alcohol and drugs, a heavy-handed approach, threats and wailing and gnashing are all likely to be counterproductive. Instead let them know that you're concerned but are there to help and not to judge.

OBESITY

At the other end of the scale altogether is the revelation by the Department of Health that 61.3 per cent of adults and 30 per cent of children aged 2–15 are overweight or obese.

Being drastically overweight is every bit as dangerous as being drastically underweight and you're at far greater risk of heart disease, certain cancers and type-2 diabetes. The NHS spends more than £6 billion every year treating patients for conditions associated with being overweight or obese.

If you are worried about your grandchild's weight, take a look at what they are eating and how much physical activity they are doing. It's fairly easy to make small but effective changes.

It's recommended that school-age children do an hour of physical activity a day. Clearly you're not going to turn a confirmed couch potato into Jessica Ennis-Hill in the space of a week, but playing in the park, walking instead of going by car, swimming and other sports are all simple ways to build up to suggested levels.

Changing the whole family's diet and cutting out junk food and sugary snacks together will make life much easier than making a child do one thing while the rest of you continue to do another.

> 'I found that Granny tucking into a big pile of veg with gusto was a great way of leading by example. And I lost a pound or two too!' **(crimplene)**

Grazing is one of the worst culprits when it comes to children putting on weight. There's a lot to be said for the family meal around the table three times a day, with a balanced diet and people getting the chance to fill up and warned not to eat between meals and spoil their appetites. It's old-fashioned, perhaps, and not always easy to manage with busy modern lives, but very good discipline.

THE WISDOM OF EXPERIENCE

Remember the whole 'age and experience bring wisdom' adage? Well, it's true. Hindsight is a marvellous thing and is one of (many) reasons why grans are so wise. Here are just a few nuggets of wisdom that gransnetters wish they'd been able to offer to their teenage selves. Keep them in mind – they may come in very handy ...

> 'Get a career and a good one and pay into a decent pension.' (susiecb)

> 'Look after the pennies and the pounds will look after themselves. Don't spend your money on rubbish, save hard and buy what you want or need, don't run up debts it will lead to trouble.' (Burgundygran)

> 'Take disappointments in your stride – they are part of life, build on the positive. Look at what you've got, not always at what you haven't got.' (olliesgran)

'Don't wear stilettos for work as you will get bunions that will bother you when you're in your sixties.' (carol)

'Mine would be: listen to yourself, don't be afraid to tell your parents what you want out of life just because you want to please them, or because you are afraid they will not take you seriously.' (GoldenGran)

'Don't try too hard to grow up – it will happen some day anyway when you aren't looking.' (annobel)

'Have more belief in yourself and don't try too hard to be forever fitting in with the crowd. Pay more attention to the pursuit of studies and less to boyfriend chasing. Share aspirations (dreams of becoming a designer) with parents ... and refuse (politely) to follow their chosen path.'(supernana)

'Focus on a career and go for it. Don't go out with men with no money and certainly don't marry one (or even two in my case). Poverty isn't romantic and love does not conquer all.' (susiecb)

'You are not a lanky, skinny, glasses-wearing four-eyes, but like a caterpillar will come out as a lovely butterfly given a few years' development. And definitely use contraceptives!' (pennysue)

'Don't sit at home wondering "what if" or "maybe not" – just go and do it. You are far more capable than you think you are.' (gally)

'Don't believe that first love is forever always. Lose the weight now – it will be much harder to do later on in life. Don't believe everything he tells you. If only someone had said those things to me ...' (divawithattitude)

CHAPTER SEVEN
DIFFERENT TYPES OF GRANDPARENTING

'I guess that love is sometimes letting go of the "ideal" dream and settling for what is possible and enjoying those possibilities to the full.' (soop)

There's no longer anything typical about the 'average' family and, for most of us, family has become a rather more fluid and interesting thing than the nuclear unit of the Janet and John era. With divorce at an all-time high, there's nothing remotely unusual about being part of a blended or extended family, its members often spread far across the globe. However, the result of this is that we often find ourselves with new challenges that were rarely faced by our own grandparents.

If this is the position you find yourself in, rest assured that you certainly aren't the only one.

HOW TO DEAL WITH BEING A LONG-DISTANCE GRANDPARENT

'I guess it is about finding different ways of being a grandma and making our time together very special.' (mamie)

More UK grandparents than ever before have grandchildren living abroad. Even within the British Isles there are many thousands of doting grans who see their favourite small people far less often than they'd like. In fact, a survey in early 2013 showed that one in three grandparents see their grandchildren just once a month or less – and for most this is mainly a question of geography. How you cope with this depends on a number of factors.

First, the actual distance: how far away do they live? If it's across the Channel or at the other end of the country, it will obviously be easier (and cheaper) to make more frequent visits than if they're the other side of the world.

Next up, finance: if ticket prices aren't a major issue for you then clearly it makes life more straightforward than having to scrape together an international airfare at the expense of something else you really need to spend the money on.

Mobility too can play a large part in long-distance visits. If you're fit and well, then it's always going to be an awful lot simpler to travel than if you need assistance or medical arrangements to be made.

But whichever situation might apply to you, missing your grandchildren can be tough. So what are the best ways to stay in touch? And how can you make your relationship a close one despite the distance?

HOW TO STAY IN TOUCH

All hail the age of modern technology and the benefits it brings. The Internet is not the same as being able to have a cuddle – no one would ever suggest that – but it *is* a massive help in keeping that bond with the grandchildren going strong.

> 'We had family in Canada when phone calls had to go through an operator and were wildly expensive. Letters took ages to arrive and flying out to visit was beyond the means of most people. Now you have wonderful Skype, and you can email and Facebook them too.'
> **(Mrsmopp)**

We may have embraced the digital revolution with huge enthusiasm, but that's not to say that letter writing no longer has its place. As children get older it can be a great way to keep in touch. It's funny how in this electronic age it now feels like a treat to get something nice in the post.

> 'We leave address stickers and stamps and when a letter arrives they get one back straight away. They are such a novelty that they are taken into school for show-and-tell!' **(stansgran)**

But if your grandchildren are too young to put pen to paper and you find you are communicating mainly online, then it can be very useful to work out a 'communications strategy' between you and your children. (Okay, so this basically means sticking good times to call in the diary – but it sounds impressively organised!) Set up an arrangement that works for you both and allows you to spend precious time chatting with the little ones. Making sure your conversations with grandchildren aren't just an add-on to your phone calls to their parents is a good start.

Time differences and various commitments can sometimes make it tricky to be in front of your computers at the same time, and it's dreadfully disappointing to keep trying without finding anyone at the other end. So pre-booking time to talk or having a regular slot that takes priority over pretty much everything else can work well (though spontaneous chats are always lovely too).

Skype and similar services (such as FaceTime, for Apple users, and Google+, which is becoming increasingly popular and, like the other services, is free to use) have revolutionised contact with loved ones who aren't close by. You can chat as long as you like without panicking about running up huge bills, and being able to see each other is not only lovely, but can also be a lot more practical with little ones who, let's face it, aren't always the most communicative of creatures. (We've all learnt that the stock answer to questions such as 'What did you do at school today?' is either 'Nothing' or 'I can't remember'.)

> 'I use Google+ to phone my son on his mobile from my computer, or it can be used computer to computer screen (it's called a hangout), and it costs nothing. When it rings the special tone, the grandkids know it's us calling! We've found glove puppets are good to use – and lots of show-and-tell – from both sides – is very popular as well.' **(butty)**

That's one of the big plusses of video calling, it offers lots of ways to make your contact even more special.

> 'I know someone who reads bedtime stories to his grandchild on Skype: he buys two copies of each story book, one for the child and one for him: they open their books together and he reads to the child.' **(joan)**

Of course little children have a habit of growing far too quickly, and if you don't see them often it can be hard to keep up with the changes. But one tip from the forums is that having local friends with children the same age as your grandchildren can be a great help in keeping you up to date with the interests of that particular age group.

Photos are invaluable. (Funny how when you have a clear-out, photographs are the one thing you never, ever want to throw away. In fact, if you're not careful and start looking at them, that will be the end of the clear-out.) But where once film and printing were expensive (especially if, like us, you took several duds on every roll), you can now take as many pictures as you like, free, and share them online.

Many people use Facebook for this, with the relevant security settings if you don't want the world to be able to see your pictures. There are also various sites such as Photobucket where you can post photos under a password so that only people who you choose can access them. Dropbox is another easy way to share files with password protection.

You can do the same with videos, plus smaller files can be sent by email and bigger ones put on DVDs or uploaded to YouTube – again, you can make them private and only allow access to those you choose.

But the sad fact is that all the online interaction in the world doesn't mean there won't be days when it all feels a bit rubbish to be so far away.

> 'We bombard them with postcards and email photos of us about our daily life so they keep the connection. We plant seeds and bulbs when they come and email photos of their progress and the children photo their drawings and email them and read to us on Skype. It is still a

> very lonely place, but a stiff upper lip is a great help.' (stansgran)

Other strategies adopted by gransnetters include playing interactive games with the grandchildren online, writing stories together (you write one paragraph and your grandchild the next) and having a special stone found and exchanged during visits, that gran and child care for. (Every time you touch it, you can think of each other and, when you speak, you can ask how 'your stone' is getting on.)

Of course some people are better communicators than others and if your child isn't great at emailing (or Skyping or phoning) it does make it harder to keep in touch with the grandchildren. It can help, as one gransnetter suggested, to have a set of 'bravery' strategies for low days and moments. But even if you have daily contact in one way or another, no one is pretending it's easy to be hundreds – even thousands – of miles from the ones you love.

> 'All my grandchildren are either in the USA or Australia. I cry quite often!' (grandmanorm)

It's important to find consolation where you can and, for many, there is a great deal of comfort in the fact that their families are happy, independent and settled and living a life they may not have been able to lead back home.

'I always encouraged my daughters to travel, see the world, seek new experiences and, guess what? They did. But I know I did a good job because they always want to come "home" as often as they can and that's what matters. Preparing for visits is always exciting, and you have to remember that they are doing what is best for them.' (gally)

IF THEY MOVE AWAY

Of course if your grandchildren have always lived far away, it's one thing. If they suddenly declare that they're upping and leaving when they currently live round the corner, it's quite another. 'We're moving abroad' is a phrase that many gransnetters dread. Probably not great for your relationship to wail and gnash teeth, though. By all means let them know how much you will miss having them around, but don't make them feel guilty about leaving. You may have to muster the skills of an Oscar-winning actress here, but it will be worth it in the end.

'Love them and let them go (but keep a small thread attached so you can haul them back again every so often!).' (greatnan)

It's worth doing your best to make the parting a positive one.

> 'My daughter and son-in-law are moving to live permanently in New Zealand next year. They really have appreciated our situation and know that we are sad and will miss them, but as they are definitely going to go I want them to feel they go with our blessing and the hope that their new life will work out well for them.' (grannyactivist)

On the bright side (and, yes, there really is a bright side), children living abroad can offer you the chance to spend holidays in places you might never otherwise have visited. For many grandparents there's also the opportunity to spend intense quality time (including bedtime, bath time and early-morning cuddles) with the little ones – a definite bonus.

But how often should you visit?

For most people this will be governed by distance and/or finance. Clearly if they are in, say, Australia and you're in the UK, you won't be popping over for regular weekends. There may be particular occasions when they really feel they need you there (to help with a new baby or offer other support), but otherwise it's just a matter of finding periods that suit you all best. How long you stay when you get there may again be governed by distance. (It's all very well Benjamin Franklin saying that guests, like fish, begin to smell after three days, but if you've crossed half the world just to get there, no one will be expecting you to pack your bags and go again within 72 hours!)

As the grandchildren get older, if the distance isn't too terrifying, you may even be able to have them to stay on their own, though you need to be sensitive about broaching this. Parents understandably worry about grandparents keeping up with high-energy small children who aren't familiar with the dangers of a new environment.

You may have fantastic, intense, fun-filled visits, but inevitably they're going to come to an end. It may be less difficult to say goodbye if everyone knows when the next trip will be.

> 'Every time we leave, or they leave us, the thought is always: "When will we see them next?" How we will manage as we get older is something I occasionally think about, but I then park it somewhere out of the way when I can't find a solution.' **(suedonim)**

CULTURAL DIFFERENCES

Something else to consider when grandchildren live abroad is that there may be cultural or language barriers to contend with.

> 'We are learning to embrace the difference in our cultures. I know it's easy to say "embrace the change" – but that is the only way to move forward with our children's life choices ... and it works.' **(butternut)**

But if your grandchild's first language is, say, French and you can't get much further than 'croissant', 'ooh la la' or 'Gérard Depardieu', it is going to make any form of communication a little more challenging.

Chances are they will speak some English at home, or be learning it at school, although children can be notoriously shy when it comes to demonstrating their skills. And, as they get older and spend more time communicating with their friends in their mother tongue, they may be more reluctant to use a language in which they feel less confident. It's certainly worth you considering taking lessons in their first language. Not only will they all appreciate the effort, but the small ones will likely take great pride in helping Granny with the basics.

> 'Another tip that you might find helpful and can be fun: my best friend is French, and although we both speak each other's language, when we really need a good natter she speaks in French and I in English (it is easier to understand a foreign language than to speak in it). Most bilingual families end up with "mash-up" words that become part of family vocabulary and with stories to go with them.' **(jackyann)**

As children get older it can also help to have them to stay on their own for a couple of weeks – the language barrier should disappear pretty quickly.

The main thing to remember in all this is that even very young children know that grandparents are special, even if they don't see them often. We rather liked the words of one gransnetter who said that 'Distance doesn't stop love'.

So, wherever they may be in the world, if you do find yourself living far from family and missing them, try to look forward to Skyping, phoning, photos and as many visits as you can.

> 'In the meantime just get on with life and involve yourself in lots of things and concentrate on any other children and grandchildren. Life is what you make it. I, an only child, moved 500 miles from my own parents when my children were very young and I know how Mum suffered from not seeing them regularly and I suffered from not having her help when I needed it, but times were different then. Now it is almost the norm for children to live far, far away and, sadly, it's just something we have to get used to.' (gally)

STEP-GRANDPARENTING

With blended families becoming ever more common, 'step' relationships are something that many – if not most – of us will encounter at some point or other.

Becoming a step-grandparent can happen in a number of ways. You might marry someone who has children and/or grandchildren and become their stepmum/step-gran – or marry someone who then takes on yours and so becomes a step-grandfather to your own grandchildren. Equally one of your own children may find a partner who already has a family.

There's also the added complication of exes who remarry or start new relationships, which can mean your own grandchildren having a 'step' to add into the mix, even if you're not directly involved. Clearly each of these situations throws up a different challenge.

If you find yourself as step-gran to your partner's grandchildren, you may feel (at least at the start) that you're not a 'proper' grandparent. Panic not – this is very common.

> 'I have a baby step-granddaughter – would love to be more involved, but as I am not the "real" grandmother sometimes feel I have to hold back. But I do try to help as much as I can – and hopefully she will enjoy my company and her grandfather's as she grows. It is what it is, and the main thing is that it is important not to wish for what we don't have, but to enjoy the families we have!' (grandmaL)

In truth, being a step-grandparent is much like being a step-parent (albeit – usually – a bit less hands-on), and there aren't really any hard and fast rules. Each relationship is different and can depend on many factors, such as how old the children are (if you 'inherit' them in their teens, it's clearly not going to be the same as if you've known them since birth), the relationship their parents have with your partner and with you and whether there are other grannies on the scene as well.

Take your cues from your partner or your stepchildren and you won't go far wrong. It doesn't have to be tricky!

> 'My husband and his first wife had been divorced many years before we met; she and I got on well and she was instrumental in ensuring I was accepted as "Grandma". I couldn't love them more if they were really mine, and they have added such joy to my life.' (gulligranny)

If you welcome an older step-grandchild into your family, it would clearly be unrealistic to expect your feelings for them to instantly be the same as the ones you have for any grandchildren you might already have – but they can grow. Advice from our forums is that, even if you don't feel the same about them at the start, treat them the same as the others and it will help the transition for you all.

If you already have stepchildren who have now decided to go forth and multiply, chances are that if you get on well with them you'll be considered to be another gran from the start, regardless of how many others there might be.

> 'I have two stepchildren, who I have known since they were six and seven years old. I love them both as if they were my own children. They have three children

between them, so far, and in everyone's eyes I am their nanny – the most important eyes being theirs! Okay, they have more nannies than some of their friends, but nannies who love you is one thing you can never have too many of! Yes, it gets complicated at Christmas and birthdays, etc., but so what?' **(divawithattitude)**

WHEN YOUR NEW PARTNER TAKES ON YOUR GRANDCHILDREN

Again, there are many permutations that will have some bearing on how this works. Does your partner have his own children or grandchildren? Does he get on with yours? Are there various exes lurking in the background?

'My husband is a sort of step-grandparent to my grandson. I say 'sort of' because my grandson still has both his genetic grandfathers. My husband does very well. I think he sees it, consciously or subconsciously, as part of the kindness he owes me, his wife. He watches my grandson with interest and is kindly and always ready to be helpful, but he does not get as involved as he might if he were directly related.' **(baggy)**

Even if all the other grandparents are on the scene, there's nothing to stop you adding an 'honorary granddad'. As one gransnetter succinctly put it, this doesn't take away any of your former partner's granddadness!

And most of us would agree that there shouldn't be a limit on any child having people to love them and look out for them.

> 'I will be forever grateful to my in-laws for welcoming my children by my first marriage (then eight and four) into their lives. In truth, they were much better grandparents than the natural paternal grandparents. They looked for things to interest the children, took them out, gave them little (not expensive) things. The children remained loyal to their natural grandparents and only ever called their step-grandparents by their first names, but they loved them – and I think in the long term, learnt very important lessons about how to be a good grandparent from them.' **(flopsybunny)**

WHEN YOUR CHILDREN TAKE ON STEPCHILDREN THEMSELVES

Once again, how old they are, how often you see them, how many other people are involved in the mix and how everyone gets on are going to be instrumental in building this new relationship. Whether or not you have your own grandchildren (and in this case, whether they are going to be living with your step-grandchildren) can also be a factor.

All the same rules apply.

Don't beat yourself up if it takes time for you to adjust to the new relationship, especially if the children are only with your son or daughter at weekends and during the holidays. Let things develop at their own pace.

Do try to treat them the same as your other grandchildren nonetheless. The less 'different' they feel, the more easily they will integrate into their new family unit.

> 'Children will always know when they are made welcome, and sometimes the ones that you have to "try harder" with are all the more special.' **(Fondasharing)**

Don't get upset if they don't want to call you 'Grandma', especially if they have other grannies around.

Don't think that because you 'inherited' each other your relationship can't be as rewarding as any other.

> 'We found ourselves with three almost grown-up grandchildren 10 years ago and I can say we have come to be very fond of them. We recently got a grandchild through our son, and one of the step-grandchildren asked us to please remember they were here first. They have all enriched our lives a lot.' **(eleanorre)**

THE EX-FACTOR

If you are separated or divorced and your ex finds a new partner, it can be a difficult adjustment, particularly if you haven't parted on good terms.

> 'I would be horrified if my grandson started calling his granddad's girlfriend 'Grandma' ... she bl**dy isn't his grandma ... that's a fact! I don't mean to sound bitter and twisted, but she didn't bring my son up. If we had split up when he was younger, I would maybe have felt differently, but as my son was in his twenties when his father and I split up she is not his stepmother, simply his dad's girlfriend.' (helshea)

It's perfectly understandable that you may feel hurt and angry, and the last thing any gran wants is to think she's being usurped. But no one can take away the relationship you have built with your grandchild – unless you let them. So, hard though it may be, don't allow your feelings to spoil the time you spend together, and don't – under any circumstances – try to influence the way your grandchild feels about 'the other woman'. These things never end well and you also risk damaging your relationship with your children, which will only make the situation worse.

> 'Sometimes you just have to grit your teeth and keep quiet about your own feelings for the sake of your relationships. Nobody says it is fair – but you have to

> ask yourself whether you want to be happy or you want to be right.' (greatnan)

Yes, three (or more!) grandmothers might technically be a crowd, but try to embrace the fact that the children are so well loved and treasure the fact that the relationship they have with you is unique.

TWIN GRANDCHILDREN

> 'Have any of you discovered yet that you can't be in charge of twins on a busy road and be able to sneeze or hold a handbag?' (carboncareful)

Double trouble perhaps, but double the fun too, at least according to the grans of twins on Gransnet. That said, if you're ever left holding the babies it can certainly be a challenge to keep up once they're on the move. If you're daunted by the prospect, take heart:

> 'As they get older, you will find they entertain each other a fair bit as well. Mainly relax and enjoy the enormous privilege of time spent with two interested and fascinating little people.' (happygran268)

But there is no doubt that it can be exhausting to have two children of the same age clamouring for attention at the same time.

> 'Sometimes it makes my head spin! I remember when they were babies and I looked after them for a couple of hours they both started crying at once and I didn't know who to pick up first! It's hard when they both want to be picked up and cuddled at the same time. I usually end up on the floor or the sofa with them, one each side, because I can't lift them both at once!' (nannyliz)

Described by one gran as 'like herding sheep', it can certainly be hard work, but it is often easier than looking after children of different ages. And (we are assured) it does get easier.

> 'Plus any exhaustion is more than compensated by the sheer joy they bring. My grandsons are mischievous and full of energy, and I would struggle to look after them every day, but I am happy to muck in and help with bath time, pick them up from the childminder occasionally and do my share of babysitting.' (carol)

Useful tips from our forums include:

- Keep bringing along packs of nappies to help out with the family budget. They go through huge amounts. Looking for nappy offers and using doubled-up Tesco (or other loyalty card) points to replenish nappy stocks can help.

- Assume your daughter/in-law will experience extreme fatigue in the first few months, so provide as many opportunities as you can for her to recharge her batteries.
- Remember that they are individuals and may have very different personalities and interests. Always use both names when calling them.
- Remember that they can help each other get into mischief: i.e. one pushing the other into the washing machine; one pushing the other up and over the gate; holding the chair for the other to climb up, etc. They can be a force to be reckoned with when they gang up on you!
- Twins often come early and if they are very small may have to spend time in the special-care baby unit. This can be daunting and worrying for you all, but the support of Mum/Gran can really make a difference.

BEING AN ADOPTIVE GRANDPARENT

'My daughter is unable to have children and is now adopting a little girl who is six and has had a pretty tough start in life. I want to be the most welcoming new granny I can be. But I don't know how accepting she will be of me, what I can do to help her settle, how to make her feel like part of the family or how to deal with all this in relation to my other grandchildren.' (linky)

It's easy to feel a little out of your depth in a situation such as this, and it's natural to be anxious about how you can help make the process easier for all involved.

You certainly can't rush it – however much you might want to – and being patient and taking time to build the relationship will stand all of you in good stead. Remember that this is an enormous change for a child who might have had a lot of difficulties to deal with in the past and it's inevitable that there will be the odd bump in the road (however small).

You can certainly help by supporting your child by spending time looking after and slowly getting to know the adopted child and by finding things that you can enjoy doing together.

Above all, be yourself. Be calm and welcoming and don't look like you are trying too hard. It will all be quite overwhelming for the child and they will need time to get to grips with who's who and what's what. Try not to push the interaction.

> 'Any activity that you can invite her to join (making cakes, rolling pastry, gardening, etc.) allows her the chance to be at your side and develop a closeness, while giving her the option not to engage if she doesn't feel ready. Don't be upset if it takes her a while, though.'
> **(inthefields)**

Do be led by the child. If they're not keen on being showered with hugs and kisses, then keep things at their pace. Likewise, if they need affection and cuddles, be there for them. The more you know about them and their background, the better you will understand them.

> 'There may be plenty of new issues to face, but they are equally challenging to those presented by growing children who aren't adopted, and the things you find yourself mulling over won't necessarily be caused by them being adopted. We've found in our family that we forget who was adopted or long-term fostered until someone outside the family reminds us for some reason. You'll find your own level – don't feel the attachment has to come all at once – you'll realise one day that there is a deep bond between you, and it feels like it was always there. How fantastic to have a much-wanted child arriving in your family.' **(whenim64)**

SPECIAL-NEEDS GRANDCHILDREN

It can be tough to accept that your grandchild has special needs – be they developmental, emotional, physical or any other. Sometimes you will know from birth, other times diagnoses can take years. Sometimes people are desperate for answers, other times people are reluctant to accept that there's anything wrong.

So what do you do if you suspect there's a problem but no one will acknowledge your concerns?

> 'My grandson is five years old and, although not officially diagnosed, I know that he is autistic, but my son will not listen to me and I'm scared if I keep mentioning that he needs to seek some advice (on parenting) he will stop talking to me and not let me see my grandson. His wife is no better, but I really need to get them to understand how they can help.' (Lyndajgran)

At this age things are made slightly easier by the fact that if the child *is* autistic this will be picked up in school and taken forward from there, with his parents' involvement. Though:

> 'Some behaviours can appear to indicate autism, but it doesn't mean that is the case, and a diagnosis or label of autism for some children is not necessarily needed in order to enable the child to progress and develop. It all depends on the degree of concern.' (whenim64)

So the best thing that you can do at this stage is be as supportive as you can. Remember that the parents may be equally worried, but reluctant to have their child saddled with a label.

After all, the bottom line is that no parent wants to be told their child has a problem – by you or anyone else –

and, even if they share your concerns, they may well be defensive and angry.

> 'I was blind to my daughter's problem for years as she was "just like her daddy" ... she was only diagnosed as an adult, when she sought the diagnosis herself. Her father remains undiagnosed, and completely unaccepting of his daughter's formal diagnosis, despite the fact that she has been participating in the Cambridge research programme.
>
> So ... what choices do you have? I think that you could push hard, but you risk losing all contact if the parents become angry enough. I am not sure that it would get you anywhere, other than alienated, as, although you absolutely have your grandchild's best interests at heart, the parents won't see it that way if they haven't realised for themselves that all is not as it should be. In their shoes, you will simply be criticising their child.' **(inthefields)**

Alternatively you can simply watch and wait and be there to support when (and if) the parents actually start to realise that there is an issue.

If there is a formal diagnosis, what is done will depend on its severity. Some children will need to attend a special school, others will continue in mainstream education. It's impossible to generalise: the spectrum is a broad one and can range from mild delayed learning to serious physical, emotional and learning problems, which can make finding the right path for the specific child very difficult.

> 'I have a grandchild with autism, and I have found that, once a professional diagnosis has been made, and appropriate support/schooling has been put in place, that I have allowed the label to float off somewhere, so that I can enjoy my delightful and funny grandchild just for who he is and for how he is.' (butty)

With milder learning difficulties some find that there are both pros and cons to diagnosis.

> 'My son was diagnosed dyspraxic when he was nine and it was useful in getting help. There was definitely something "different" about him as a child, but there's little sign of it now and he doesn't regard himself as dyspraxic any more. His brain just worked a bit differently, he feels, and that lessened or became less obvious as he got older. So, what I'm saying, I suppose, is that it's important not to let the diagnosis define the child – it may give you some clues, but it's going to be a vague explanation at best.' (GranIT)

If your grandchild is diagnosed with any type of special needs, disability or health condition, you may find yourself not only having to deal with your own emotions, but supporting their parents through it all too. They may need practical help, such as looking after other children while they are at appointments or a bit of respite care, or they may simply need someone to talk to or a shoulder to cry on. Offer to help; don't wait to be asked. Little things like going along to hospital appointments can make it less lonely and daunting for the parents and make a real difference.

If a diagnosis comes unexpectedly at birth, remember that the parents will be shell-shocked and will need a lot of emotional support as they deal with the news on top of everything else that goes with having a brand-new baby. You are all likely to be going through a whole range of emotions, ranging from joy to sadness, anger to disbelief and grief. These are all absolutely normal, and it isn't 'wrong' to experience any of them. However, if you are busy trying to look after everyone else, do make sure you also allow yourself time to come to terms with it all.

New babies are notorious for eating up attention at the best of times – and never more so when there is a problem. If there are other grandchildren, make sure that you find time for them too. They need to know that they still matter just as much as the new addition (which, of course, they do – though it is difficult to explain to a toddler why their sibling is getting all the fuss).

In the longer term, it can be helpful to keep up to date with what's happening with your grandchild, especially if you don't see them often. If you are going to be looking after them, it's useful to find out as much as you can about their condition. It can all be a bit daunting, and a little knowledge can give you a lot more confidence. It can also mean the parents are a lot happier to leave your grandchild in your care – they may well be reluctant to leave them with anyone else. You'll also be more clued up about any special equipment they may need when they come to visit.

It's always worth remembering that there are support groups for many conditions such as Down's syndrome, cystic fibrosis, cerebral palsy and many, many more. These can offer the whole family a chance of talking with others, learning more and finding the help you need.

BEING A GRANDPARENT WITH A DISABILITY

Most grandparents are only too keen to help out with their precious grandchildren whenever they can. For a gran with physical limitations there's always the worry about what you *aren't* able to do, but even if you can't help with practical tasks such as dressing, changing and bathing you can still do the most important thing of all by offering your love and emotional support. Oh, and never underestimate the power of cuddling!

You can also sing to the baby or perhaps rock the pram while Mum is making up a bottle – a very necessary part of being a grandma!

And, whatever your concerns about the things you can't do, you will find that somehow these things usually have a way of working themselves out.

'I couldn't carry the baby about but I was excellent at "burping" (in fact my left shoulder is "the magic shoulder"!). I couldn't lean over the bath – or even support Baby in the baby bath on the table – but I gave an excellent cuddle to swaddled Baby while Mummy dried her own hands, etc. before dressing her. Even now I don't race around a playground with my granddaughter, but I can and do manage crafting/baking activities and I read great bedtime stories with all the different voices! So, basically, my advice is don't worry too much about what you may be UNable to do. Time will sort out for you all the exciting things which you WILL be able to do and you will love every minute!' **(Heather)**

BEING A PARENT AS WELL AS A GRANDPARENT

Women having babies later, second marriages, blended families and all the other changes we've seen become commonplace over the last generation or two have all contributed to the fact that it's no longer a rarity for people to become grandparents while they still have younger children living at home.

> 'I have a daughter of five and I am about to have my first grandchild. My older daughter is keen for me to help with childcare. I don't mind, but I wonder if I will feel I don't have as much right to direct my grandchild's behaviour as my younger daughter's? Does anyone have any advice about how to make this work?' **(hokeypokey)**

Advice? Of course! That's the wisdom of grans for you.

If you're looking after children and grandchildren of similar ages, it's likely they'll end up with something more like a sibling relationship than that of uncle/aunt and nephew/niece, but that's no bad thing unless there's a clash about how the children are brought up.

> 'I have two children in their 30s and a son of 11 – and my grandchildren are 9 and 4. It all works very well for us. I often have my grandson to stay, as my daughter and son-in-law have a business, and she reciprocates by having her brother to stay if we want to go out or have a weekend away. Our boys are all very close. Though I will reprimand my grandson if necessary, I am probably stricter with my son as I feel it is the parent's responsibility to bring up their boys as they wish. I think my grandson views my son almost as an older brother and he in turn is very close to his older siblings.' **(seasider)**

CHAPTER EIGHT
DIFFICULT SITUATIONS

HELPING GRANDCHILDREN TO COPE WITH BEREAVEMENT

Death, naturally, is something we all want to shield our grandchildren from for as long as we can. But, inevitably, it's just not always possible.

DEATH OF A PET

For many children the first experience of bereavement is the loss of a pet. It seems several gransnetters – like us – had mothers who simply flushed a dear departed goldfish down the lavatory 'to join its friends in the sea'. (And, yes, we fell for it hook, line and sinker and moved happily on.) But, given you can't cuddle or groom a goldfish, it's possibly easier to cope with this than the death, say, of a cat that's slept on the end of your bed every night or a dog you have taken for walks or even a rabbit or hamster you've enjoyed playing with.

Those of us who have lost much-loved pets as adults know that it can be a devastating blow, and for children it's no different. The advice from our forums is:

- *Don't* belittle the loss.
- *Don't* suggest getting another one simply to 'replace' the lost pet.

> 'You can't just replace a beloved dog as you would replace a broken toy.' (yogagran)

- Encourage the child to do something to remember their pet – be it a special picture or painting, or creating an area in the garden. They will often find great comfort in this and it offers a good opportunity for them to talk.
- Be honest. Don't try to sanitise what happened by saying something along the lines of 'He just went to sleep'. This is likely to leave children panicking every time any other pets shut their eyes and may even make them believe that if they go to sleep they might not wake up either.
- Let the child know that it's absolutely fine and normal to feel sad.

'As with all deaths that children have to cope with, let them deal with it how they want to. If it's having a cry and a cuddle, then be there for them. If they want to talk, then listen. You won't have to say much, in fact it's probably best just to acknowledge their feelings and add the odd soothing word. Just be there as a safe haven for them to cry or talk.' (HildaW)

DEATH OF A FRIEND OF FAMILY MEMBER

When it's a relative or friend that dies, although the loss will be incalculably larger, the principles in dealing with it are much the same.

Most young children go through a stage where they ask constant questions about death and being honest (you don't have to be graphic or alarmist!) is key. Why do people die? Why are they buried? Perfectly normal questions. Just keep your answers simple and truthful.

'Children understand far more than we often give them credit for, and death is as much a part of living as life is.' (sook)

If you have religious beliefs, the idea of heaven and angels can be a comforting one, even if it can lead to the odd tricky discussion with an inquisitive child.

'Granddaughter, aged four: "If we go to heaven when we die, how come all the skeletons live in the churchyard?"

Cue my flustered explanation about souls and not needing old bones any more that didn't even sound convincing to myself.' (marionh)

There are some lovely books available to help children through the process of bereavement and you may find it easier to use one as a starting point for any conversations rather then trying to work out where to begin yourself. Either way:

- *Don't* try to be too strong. Not only will it do you no good to bottle up or try to hide your feelings, but it's also important for the children to know you feel sad too and that you can help each other get through it.
- *Don't* let them think that they can't talk about it. They need to know that they can do so whenever they want or need to without worrying that they are upsetting you by bringing the subject up. Likewise, don't hide away photos – use them to keep their loved ones in their memories.
- It's obvious, of course, but the age of the child will govern how you explain what's happened. Smaller children are often happy with the idea that Granddad (for example) is up in heaven and looking out for them or that he is now a star twinkling down on them as they sleep, but older children will want to know more.

'When my husband died last year, all the grandchildren were told in different ways, according to their level of understanding. The three-year-old talks of him often, along with our dog, who died shortly before. She thinks they live on a cloud and play on the beach as they always used to. When she flies, she waves out of the window to them, much to the amusement of other passengers. All the children are surrounded by photos of him and he comes up in conversations very often. Reassurance is paramount. They are all used to seeing us cry and can be comforting when this happens and not fazed by it. Just be yourselves.' (gally)

- Like grown-ups, children will experience a whole range of emotions after the death of someone they love, including anger, disbelief, guilt, shock and sadness. It is not unusual for these feelings to come and go and, while they may seem fine about it all one moment, they may find it hard going later on. This is very normal.
- It's important to help them realise the finality of death and that the person is gone forever. This can be very difficult for small children – indeed any of us – to grasp.
- You need to help them understand that none of this is down to them. Children often pinpoint something they have done wrong and start to worry that somehow this may have precipitated the death. Again, this is not unusual, but it's essential you reassure them that none of this is their fault.

- As part of this, it's also a good idea to explain why the person died.

  'We told our grandson that Grandad was too ill for the doctors to make him better in hospital so he went to the moon. Grandad has become the man in the moon in his eyes and he says goodnight to him each night and tells him he loves him.' (lindylooby)

Children may well ask if they are going to die too. Explain to them that everyone will die some time, but that most people don't die until they are very old (of course if they think you are very old – and sometimes anything over 30 seems positively ancient – there may well then be concern from them about your own future). Be reassuring and accept that bereavement means that many children become clingy for a while afterwards. It's a natural part of the process and their worries are perfectly normal. Being there when they want to talk or just need a hug will help a lot.

When it comes to the funeral, explain that it's a chance for people – usually grown-ups – to say goodbye. If there aren't going to be any children present, there's no reason why they can't create a special goodbye of their own. Some religions (such as Judaism) do not allow anything to be placed in the coffin before burial, but, if there are no constraints, children can find it helpful to draw a picture, write a letter or find a little gift so that the relative or friend has something special to take to heaven to remember them by.

Some people do like to allow children to attend the funeral, but it's a very personal decision and a lot will depend on the age of the child, how they have reacted to the death, how much they understand about what happens at the service and how they are likely to cope. It's worth remembering that there may well be very distressed adults at the cemetery and this can be difficult and confusing for a child to deal with.

If a child is coming along, perhaps find a small role to give them a focus for the occasion, such as lighting a candle (with a grown-up's help) or laying a posy on the coffin. Do help them to understand that it will be a sad event but you can also spend time remembering happy things about the person who died.

WHEN YOU DON'T GET ON WITH A GRANDCHILD

As George Orwell wrote in his novel *Animal Farm*: 'All animals are equal, but some are more equal than others.' And, for some, this applies just as neatly to grandchildren. They might – usually secretly, occasionally openly – have a favourite. Or they might have one that they just don't click with as well as the others.

'My mother had definite favourites – my brother and her first grandchild – and had no problem voicing this.

It used to make me mad and made me determined to always be absolutely fair in all things family. I suppose one could admit to having a better connection with a certain child, but they should know that they are equally loved.' (shysal)

But what happens if – despite your best efforts – you don't get on with a grandchild?

'One of my grandsons does not like me and is either rude to me or ignores me. I try very hard not to take it to heart and feel ridiculous I am letting a six-year-old child get to me. I can't think of anything I have done to alienate him – he's not the oldest or the youngest grandchild or anything. His parents do admonish him and I feel now he dislikes me more because he has been told not to be so rude to me. It has been like this since he was three.' (basing23)

There's no doubt it's very hurtful and upsetting if a grandchild you adore doesn't return your feelings, but (particularly with little ones) this does tend to be a phase, albeit one that can last a fair while.

Lots of children go through a stage of worshipping Mum and Dad:

'And heaven help anyone who they think is trying to take their place, even in the smallest way.' (jangly)

As they get older, the situation usually improves. In the meantime, carry on treating the child exactly as you treat your other grandchildren, show them you love them without making a big deal of it and play the waiting game. Rudeness should not be accepted at any time though, and if you feel it best to rope Mum and Dad in for a telling-off then do so.

If the change is a sudden one, it may that something tiny or utterly trivial has been taken too much to heart without you realising. One gransnetter discovered that her simple instruction to stop playing with the Wii rankled so much that she was excommunicated for months on end without realising why.

> 'My grandchildren are not allowed videos on while we are visiting, so I have been asked, "Are you going home now?"' (harrigran)

Grandchildren can also behave like this because there's something else going on in their lives. For example, attention is being deflected by a new sibling so this is their way of redirecting it back to them, or there may be something that's worrying them that they just don't know how to deal with.

Sometimes peer-group influence at school may make children (often boys) believe that it's 'cool' to be offhand or rude and 'babyish' to show affection. Oh, and then there is adolescence, when even the sweetest of children can turn into surly teenagers able only to communicate in grunts and shrugs.

Don't try too hard to win them over or pester them to find out what the problem is – odds are that a bit of space and the reassurance that you still care will make them come round in time.

> 'When my eldest grandson was six he decided he didn't like me and it was very tempting to overdo it in every way to "win back" his affection. Instead I didn't make any fuss at all of him. It was very hard to keep a cool head and not grab him in a big hug or even constantly defer to him, but I kept it up. After a couple of weeks I noticed a distinct thawing on his part. It may not work for everyone, but it certainly worked for me.'
> (GrandmaAnge)

HELPING CHILDREN COPE WITH DIVORCE

According to the latest figures from the Office for National Statistics, around 42% of marriages in the UK are expected to end in divorce. Which means it's highly likely that relationship breakdown is something your grandchildren are likely to encounter in some form or other.

IF YOU DIVORCE

If you and your husband have decided to divorce, it's one thing telling your adult children, but how on earth do you explain to the little ones that Granny and Granddad won't be living together any more?

The best way to do it is to tell them together. That way you can both reassure them that your feelings for them will not change in any way and that both of you will be there for them as before. If you are already estranged, or if the parting is acrimonious, then this may be out of the question. Nonetheless, even if you are telling them without your ex being present, do put your own feelings aside to assure the children that both of you love them deeply and that is not going to change.

You should also make sure that you leave yourselves plenty of time to answer any questions the children might have.

> 'It was so tempting to blurt it out on the doorstep then run away to lock myself away with a bottle of wine and a wad of tissues. But I knew that they would want to know how it was going to work, that I was okay and most of all that they would see us (both of us ... deep breaths ...) as much as before even if it wasn't together. It did help to do it properly. But the bottle of wine definitely came in handy afterwards.'
> **(ladle)**

Be honest. There is no point pretending that everything is going to be the same when it isn't.

Be slightly less honest about any failings your ex might have had. He's still their grandfather and, although it's now up to him to maintain his relationship with the children, allow him to do so without bitterness. This may well require several bottles of wine and a huge amount of teeth gritting, but it is absolutely the right thing to do.

Older children may have more questions – and if there is a third party involved they are more likely to grasp the mechanics of the break-up whatever you omit in the detail. But tempting though it is to bad-mouth your ex, it may well backfire on you, so focus instead on the positive relationships you have with your children and grandchildren rather than the one that has ended. It's fine for them to understand that you are sad that you are divorcing, but do avoid sharing too much emotion with them. They will have plenty to deal with themselves.

Unless you are parting as friends, it's best to stay out of the relationship your ex has with your grandchildren in future. Do your best to make things as easy as you can for the little ones. The last thing you want is a five-year-old panicking that their birthday party is going to be ruined by his grandparents throwing teacups at one another.

No one is saying it's going to be easy to turn up at a wedding, christening or a family party and come face-to-face with the person you used to be married to – especially if one has a new partner and the other is yet to move on – but immerse yourself in the company of your darling grandchildren and chances are you'll find yourself smiling.

IF YOUR CHILDREN DIVORCE

> 'Someone once said to me that in this scenario a grandparent's house should be the place where they feel safe and loved. A vacuum without any of the tension coming from their parents. You're their comfort blanket.' **(crimson)**

It can be devastating to hear that one of your children's marriages has broken up – especially if you hadn't seen the split coming.

> 'I thought they were the perfect couple.' **(GrandmaH)**

You worry about your son or daughter. If you have a good relationship with your son- or daughter-in-law, you will be worrying about them too, and also how this may affect things between you in future. And, of course, you will worry enormously about the effect the divorce will have on your grandchildren.

If it's a mutual decision and there's no third party involved, it often makes it easier for everyone to stay on good terms. And there are, of course, a million reasons why a marriage might go wrong.

> 'Divorce happens and it often isn't one person's fault but both people are at fault.' (dorsetpennt)

It's natural to want to support your own child, but if they have caused the break-up it's not always easy. And however well you have always got on with your daughter-in-law in the past, if your son has, for example, broken up the marriage by having an affair, then this is going to test your relationship to the limits. It's not the death knell by any means – she may well acknowledge your support and appreciate your love and the fact you are not taking sides – but equally she may be angry enough to want to hurt you for no other reason than that you're his mum.

Be as friendly and supportive as you can and keep your relationship with your grandchildren on as normal a footing as possible – for them as well as you. They are having to adjust to huge changes in their lives, so some consistency and solidity is invaluable – as is an objective ear when they need to talk.

We know of many happy lifelong relationships between former mothers- and sons-/daughters-in-law, despite the fact that the marriage has not lasted. It might take a bit of effort, but it's absolutely worth it, not least because it will make things an awful lot easier for the small folk.

Oh, and if and when another relationship develops, don't forget that:

'There's a fine balance to tread, being welcoming to the new person and not making them feel you prefer the first partner, but also remembering the first partner may feel ousted if you are friendly to the new partner. Bit of a minefield!' **(carol)**

In terms of helping your grandchildren through the split, these are some of the top dos and don'ts from our forums:

- Let them know how loved they are and offer lots of hugs, laughter and warmth.
- Remind them that *both* parents love them (even if you are not getting on with one or other) and that they are in no way to blame for the split.
- Keep things relaxed and cheerful to remind them that your home is consistently welcoming and a place to put worries aside for a while. Familiar activities can be a great distraction.
- Make sure you never put them in a position where they have to choose where their loyalties lie.
- Offer them a quiet space to talk, without asking any leading questions. Try drawing them out gently with: 'Do you know why you feel sad?' or 'What's worrying you?', etc.
- If they ask direct questions (for example, 'Why did Daddy go off and leave Mummy?'), don't get into specifics, but do reassure them that neither Mummy nor Daddy will leave *them*.

'In particular you should let them know that their granny is not going anywhere and will always be there for them. That is the one promise you can make with certainty.' (Granny23)

When looking to the future, remember that it's obviously best for everyone – including you – to keep things as amicable as possible. Even if that just can't be done, continue to do what you can to be supportive, objective and welcoming to both sides.

'Statistics show that paternal grandparents are more likely to be denied contact with their grandchildren if there is dispute/separation between parents. When they are babies we never imagine this can happen, but some of us know this heartbreak. So, grandparents, don't rock the boat at an early stage.' (maniac)

IF YOU ARE DENIED CONTACT WITH YOUR GRANDCHILDREN

'Grandparents don't necessarily do anything wrong to be denied access – but they are useful pawns to hurt when one parent or the other wants to wreak revenge or exert control.' (carol)

The last thing that any grandparent ever wants is to be denied the opportunity to see or speak to a precious grandchild. But – unhappily – it does happen. More than 1 million children in the UK are estranged from their grandparents, and the sad fact is that those grandparents have no formal legal rights to change the situation.

Under Section 8 of the Children Act of 1989, grandparents do have the right to ask for permission from the family court to make an application for contact. A grandparent does not have an automatic right to make an application. Involving the court is usually the last resort, and if there is any feasible way of making things better without involving lawyers, it's always advisable to take it.

It's up to parents to decide how to bring up their child and who their child spends time with, but sometimes when a marriage or partnership fails the wishes of one parent will not be upheld by the other. This is when contact with grandparents suffers or is stopped.

'After my son's divorce I saw less of my grandson – but for over a year now I, my son and family have been denied all contact with my grandson, due to conflict between my son and his ex. It's been a heartbreaking year for me but even more so for my son, who at times has felt suicidal. He's been to court, but is still denied contact because of lies. Dads have few rights. Grandparents have no rights. I have seen my MP, had a

> letter from Hon. Michael Gove MP – sympathetic, but little hope of a change in the near future.' **(maniac)**

Clearly it's not in any child's best interests to be used as a bargaining tool or ammunition in a bitter feud – whatever the cause. Every child has a right to family life (Article 8, European Convention on Human Rights). Most people would believe that a child has the right to enjoy a relationship with other family members, particularly those to whom they are close, and when this is denied it can be damaging to them as well as devastating for their grandparents.

> 'Both morally and legally, the situation is not about grandparents' rights but about the child's right to have a full and meaningful relationship with all members of his or her family while growing up. Children are not the property of parents but little people in their own right, and different generations have so much to offer.' **(nightowl)**

If contact is being restricted or denied, it's worth trying to point out to the child's full-time carer the benefits that your loving relationship will have for the child (and the collateral benefit to the parent). If this fails, you can try mediation (where an independent third party will help you all to make an agreement about access/contact), but only if both parents are willing to enter the process.

If you can't get the agreement of both parents, then you essentially have two options: you can sit it out in the hope that something will change; or you can go ahead and make an application to court for permission to apply for a court order, known as a Contact Order. If you go with the latter, it's always worth remembering that, even if successful, chances are it's not going to do much for harmonious relations with the relevant parent/s in future. You do not need a solicitor to make an application to court; courts are well used to family members acting in person.

If you do choose to apply for access (known as a Contact Order), the court will consider whether it's in the best interests of the child based on several factors, set out in what is known as the welfare checklist at Section 1(3) of the Children Act 1989. If either parent objects to your application, then it may well go to a full hearing, including oral evidence from both sides.

The situation will be evaluated by a social worker from the Children and Family Court Advisory and Support Service (CAFCASS) and then they will make recommendations to the court. The magistrates or judge do not have to follow the recommendation of the CAFCASS officer – the decision is that of the court. And:

'Even if contact is awarded to you by the court, the parents can still be very difficult over actually allowing you to have contact with the child. Disobeying a court order is, of course, contempt of court, but courts are very reluctant to give a custodial sentence to the parents because of the effect on the child/ren. Disputes in the family courts are always difficult, and I really think that, if at all possible, you should try to negotiate with the parents, rather than going down the legal route, but, of course, what you decide to do is up to you.' (nananina)

The process can be tough; it can also be expensive. If you are prepared (and able) to go to these lengths, you should remember that every aspect of your life may be assessed to show that you have had continued, beneficial contact with the children and/or can offer something to them that improves their well-being.

'It's heartbreaking to deal with, knowing that you have to toe the line and behave appropriately at all times because this will be examined by a court in due course, and might be seen negatively if you are accused of bringing a child back a few minutes late or saying something out of turn. We now have a happy boy in our midst again. It shows that you should never give up – keep plugging away with the best interests of your grandchild at heart, and examine your conscience the whole time – are you doing this for you or for the child? I know we benefit ten times over, and it is wonderful to be with him again, but I would have stayed back if I thought for one moment this was not what my grandson wanted or needed.' (carol)

Whichever path you choose to take, do try to keep all lines of communication open; everything becomes infinitely more difficult for all involved when these break down. Other things that gransnetters have found useful include:

- Set up a (non-confrontational!) blog or Facebook page. If letters and cards are not passed on or your emails and texts are blocked, if your grandchildren are old enough to use a computer, then this is a way for you to post family news and other thoughts for them to see.

'Children always google their own name at some stage, so if you have set a blog up it will appear.' (JaneEJackson)

- If you have any contact at all with the children and they are old enough to remember what you say, remind them gently how much you love them and want to continue seeing them and will always try your hardest to do that.
- However hard it may be, don't allow the feelings of anger and sadness to take over.

'Sometimes that black hole beckons, but I owe it to my granddaughter to keep fighting.' (JaneEJackson).

- It can be very difficult to rebuild your life – find support where you can, be it from friends, family, local groups (or, of course, Gransnet, where you can talk to many people who are in, or have been through, similar situations).

'The last words from one of my grandchildren were: "Mama, Mama please don't go, I will never see you again". She was six at the time. Later in the schoolyard she said, "I love you so much Mama, but I am not allowed to speak to you any more!" Horrendous. Without my friends and my dog, I think that I would have had a nervous breakdown, but I won't let my son-in-law beat me down.' **(sue)**

- Play by the rules at all times. Try everything you can think of, and record every single thing that is done to prevent access, then present it to whomever will listen.
- If you are denied contact with your grandchildren because you have become estranged from your son or daughter, try writing a letter (a pen and paper letter rather than an email). Say that you love him/her so much and that you are so sad about not keeping in touch with the grandchildren (but don't overdo this – it will come over as needy). Don't refer back to why you fell out. Do ask if you can make a fresh start.

- Many gransnetters have found it helpful to continue to write and send gifts, even if there is no response in return.

> 'Regardless of anything else, I am and will always be, a mother and granny. So, unless I'm asked not to, I shall carry on sending them things for birthdays, Easter, Christmas, etc. It sends a message that my door is always open and I'm not going to give up on my role. I don't address past issues, just keep on sending my best wishes and hope that one day there will be a breakthrough.' (grannyactivist)

- If you feel like you are the one making all the concessions (and often this is the case), try to bite your tongue and console yourself with the fact you are doing all this for your grandchildren and the benefit they will have from having you in their lives.
- Set up a savings account in their name. When they are eventually old enough to be able to contact you independently, they will know that you have been thinking about them and doing your best for them throughout their childhood.

And finally this, from one gransnetter who had been estranged from her daughter and grandchildren:

> 'While I firmly believe that my son-in-law is behind this alienation, that is not important to me. What is

important is that my daughter knows that, no matter what I have been subjected to, I will not judge her and I am here for her. I have not put her under any pressure nor made her feel guilty, something I know that I did at the beginning of all of this. I have now let her go in my mind, and thoughts of them do not occupy my every waking moment, as before. This has helped. I feel that she is coming back to me, albeit slowly. Stay strong, be patient.' (sue)

CHAPTER NINE
POSTSCRIPT

THE LAWS OF GRANSNET

When looking after small children, useful things to know include:

1. Table manners are very subjective and, yes, fingers can do the job of forks.
2. Food as a hat is a clever fashion statement.
3. Swear words may not be generally acceptable, but playing down their importance in ordinary conversation is.
4. Searing assessment of (a) your clothes and (b) your weight are perfectly okay, however cruelly accurate.
5. You need to offer the same kind of enthusiastic enjoyment of your grandchildren going on the slide

and then the swings at the park for the hundredth time on the trot as if it were the first time.

6. Likewise knock-knock jokes with dubious punchlines are as hysterically funny to you as they are to your grandchildren (at every telling).
7. There is no point in reasoning why an eight-year-old wants to wear striped leggings with a yellow floral top. If it's his choice, go with it.
8. The dog also needs to look at whatever has landed in the toilet.
9. It is fine to have a temper tantrum if Grandma switches off the TV, but Grandma is not allowed to get cross if a three-year-old does it.
10. All 15 cushions on the sofa are for the den and adults must sit with none.
11. When washing your hands, the dog's water bowl is as good as the sink.
12. You may well find yourself watching *Grandpa in my Pocket*, *Humf* or *Peppa Pig* even after the cherubs have gone home. Wise not to mention this in conversation.
13. Cheddars dipped in custard are yummy on a 'one for you and one for me' basis at mealtimes.
14. Mr Tumble and Grandad Tumble and Aunt Polly are not the same person.
15. But, yes, there are small people living inside the television.
16. Wearing lovely new boots to bed is fine (as long as no one tells Mummy).

17. There is always space for pudding, no matter whether they're too full to finish their sausages/fish fingers.
18. 'One more' book can be an infinite number.
19. Colouring is much more useful than breakfast.
20. Wellies are fine for the house.
21. You cannot see a small child when they are hiding especially not when they peek out from behind the sofa (but you will find them when they want you to).
22. Any roadside vegetation or wall is a good place to pee if you're potty-training.
23. On which note – you can throw a soiled pair of underpants away if you can't face washing them.
24. It's fine to be sent out of the bathroom when your grandchild is pooing, but accept that it is necessary to be watched while you do it.
25. No matter how tired and emotional the three-year-old is, Grandma will still be waiting for a cuddle.

(With thanks to GrandmaAnge, carol, bigburd, Ariadne, gracesmum, JessM, kittylester.)

USEFUL CONTACTS

Adfam
www.adfam.org.uk
Supporting families affected by drugs and alcohol

Bullying UK
www.bullying.co.uk
Offering advice and support on bullying

CAFCASS
www.cafcass.gov.uk
The Children and Family Court Advisory and Support Service

ChildLine
www.childline.org.uk
A private and confidential service for children and young people up to the age of nineteen, offering counselling online or on the phone

Frank
www.talktofrank.com
Friendly, confidential advice about drugs

Gransnet
www.gransnet.com
The go-to website for Britain's 14 million grandparents

Gransnet Local
local.gransnet.com
Local Gransnet sites across the UK

Kidscape
www.kidscape.org.uk
Working to provide individuals and organisations with the practical skills and resources necessary to keep children safe from harm

Mumsnet
www.mumsnet.com
The UK's top parenting site: advice for parents by parents

NSPCC
www.nspcc.org.uk
The National Society for the Prevention of Cruelty to Children

The Lullaby Trust
www.lullabytrust.org.uk
Safer sleep for babies and support for families

ACKNOWLEDGEMENTS

With huge thanks to Cari Rosen for putting this book together. Thanks too to Geraldine Bedell and the Gransnet team, especially Lara Crisp, Kat Bradley and Josie Thaddeus-Johns. Big thanks to Justine Roberts, Katie O'Donovan, Jane Gentle and everyone at Mumsnet for support, and to Liz Reeve for advice. And to everyone at Ebury, including Susanna Abbott, Catherine Knight, Alexandra Cooper and Ellie Rankine. Thanks most of all to the gransnetters, who keep us entertained and informed and (more or less) behaving ourselves, and who make being part of Gransnet so much fun and so endlessly interesting.

INDEX